The Soviet Union after Brezhnev

The Soviet Union after Brezhnev

Edited by Martin McCauley

Assisted by Simon Franses, Jackie Lyman and Tim Parsloe

Heinemann Educational Books · London

Holmes & Meier Publishers, Inc. · New York

Published in Great Britain 1983 by
Heinemann Educational Books Ltd

First published in the United States of America 1983 by
Holmes & Meier Publishers, Inc.
IUB Building
30 Irving Place
New York, N.Y. 10003

British Library Cataloguing in Publication Data

The Soviet Union after Brezhnev.
　　I. Soviet Union—Politics and government—1953—
　　I. McCauley, Martin
　　947.085'3　　　　DK274

ISBN 0-435-83478-9
ISBN 0-435-83479-7 Pbk

Library of Congress Cataloging in Publication Data

Main entry under title:

The Soviet Union after Brezhnev.

　　Based on a series of seminars held at the School of
Slavonic and East European Studies, University of London,
Jan. 1981–May 1982.
　　Includes index.
　　Contents: Preface/Simon Franses, Jackie Lyman, and
Tim Parsloe—The post-Brezhnev era/Martin McCauley—Leadership
and the succession struggle/Martin McCauley—Dissent, opposition,
and instability/Iain Elliott—(etc.)
　　1. Soviet Union—Politics and government—1953– —Addresses,
essays, lectures.　2. Soviet Union—Foreign relations—1975–
—Addresses, essays, lectures.　3. Soviet Union—Economic conditions—
1976– —Addresses, essays, lectures.　I. McCauley, Martin.　II. University
of London. School of Slavonic and East European Studies.
DK274.S651962　　　1983　　　320.947　　　83-12956
ISBN 0-8419-0918-0
ISBN 0-8419-0919-9 (Pbk.)

Phototypesetting by Inforum Ltd, Portsmouth
Printed in Great Britain by Biddles Ltd, Guildford, Surrey

Contents

Maps and Tables

The Contributors

Jonathan Alford, International Institute for Strategic Studies
Iain Elliot, Brighton Polytechnic
Simon Franses, School of Slavonic and East European Studies, University of London
Philip Hanson, University of Birmingham
Christina Holmes, Royal Institute of International Affairs
Jackie Lyman, School of Slavonic and East European Studies, University of London
Martin McCauley, School of Slavonic and East European Studies, University of London
Alec Nove, University of Glasgow
Tim Parsloe, School of Slavonic and East European Studies, University of London
George Schöpflin, London School of Economics and the School of Slavonic and East European Studies, University of London
Hugh Seton-Watson, School of Slavonic and East European Studies, University of London
Alan H. Smith, School of Slavonic and East European Studies, University of London

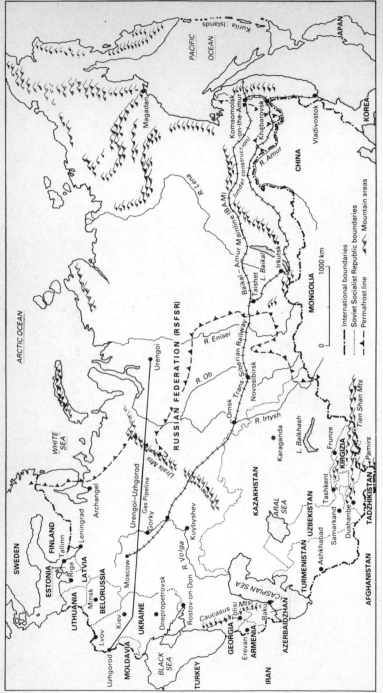

Map 1 The Soviet Union and the East

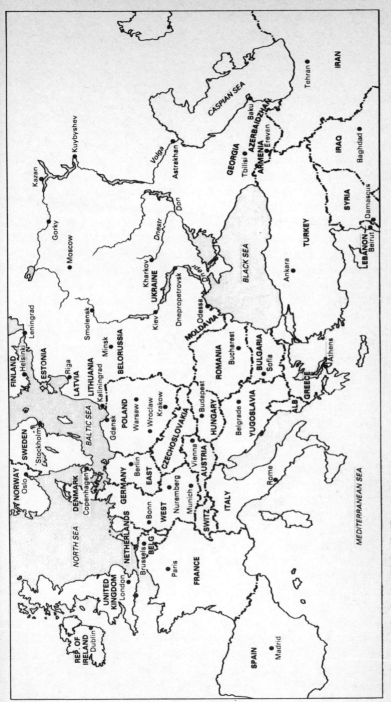

Map 2   The Soviet Union in Europe

Preface
Simon Franses, Jackie Lyman and Tim Parsloe

World affairs make the Soviet Union a focal point of interest. With this in mind, the primary aim of this book is to provide a readable analysis of current developments written by people with a broad knowledge of the Soviet system. In order to give a comprehensive picture, contributions dealing with both domestic and foreign policy have been included. Furthermore, recent events, for example the death of Brezhnev, the poor agricultural performance, deteriorating relations between East and West, and the growth of the nuclear arsenal, have led the contributors to give an informed indication of what they see as likely to happen in the remainder of the 1980s. As a result, we feel that the book will be of benefit to a wide range of readers, including business and commercial circles, as well as students.

The book has emerged from a series of seminars organised by students and held at the School of Slavonic and East European Studies, University of London. The series was planned in June 1980 and commenced with a seminar given by George Schöpflin on Soviet–East European relations (Chapter 8) in January 1981. The series extended through to May 1982, when Alec Nove spoke on Soviet agriculture (Chapter 5).

The seminars attracted members of the public and journalists, as well as students from the whole of the University of London, and were deemed of sufficient interest to warrant publication. Unfortunately, limited space has meant that some topics covered in the seminars have not been reproduced here. Nevertheless, we feel that a broad spectrum of subjects has been included. Obviously, the lecture style has been modified to a certain degree to avoid overlaps and give a thematic continuity to the book. All the contributions were received between February and July 1982.

Throughout the project, much of the organisation and work has been undertaken by students. A great deal has been learned, particularly from the members of the School staff. We hope this will encourage other students to pursue similar projects.

Finally, there are a number of people whose help and hard work have proved invaluable to the success of this book; the first and foremost being the Director of the School, Michael Branch, for his effort, encouragement and advice. We should also like to thank, in addition to the editor and contributors, Peter Ashworth, Cornelius O'Boyle and Joan Thompson. With such an extensive list of people involved, it is the editor and his assistants who must accept responsibility for any errors that may still remain.

November 1982

1 The Post-Brezhnev Era
Martin McCauley

Leonid Brezhnev died on 10 November 1982, but the announcement of his death was withheld from the Soviet and international public until 11 November. The same day, a funeral commission was formed headed by Yuri Andropov. This was the first clear sign that Andropov and his supporters were better organised than Konstantin Chernenko and his men. A day later, Andropov was elected Secretary General of the Central Committee (CC) of the Communist Party of the Soviet Union at a special CC plenum. The speed with which Andropov took over was in marked contrast to the slow pace of decision-making during the last years of Brezhnev's rule. However, Andropov, at 68 years of age, is the oldest man ever to have been elected to lead the party and is a full ten years older than Brezhnev was when he assumed party leadership in October 1964.

Does this mean that the new Soviet leadership should be viewed as an interim leadership, one which is unlikely to survive the 1980s? Will the new leaders settle for consensus, or will they attempt solutions to some of the Soviet Union's pressing problems? Is it likely that the younger generation of leaders, held back so frustratingly long by Brezhnev's tenacious hold on power, will now be able to force their way to the forefront? Or will those who feel that a thoroughgoing economic reform, high on the agenda of the new leadership, could imperil their power and privileges be able to render such a reform, and all other changes, void? Will the conflict of generations merely mean a continuation of Brezhnev's policy of muddling through?

It is worth looking at the evolution of the Soviet political system before attempting to analyse the present and see into the future.

When the Bolsheviks seized power in October 1917, a majority of the population was in favour of revolution. It soon became clear that Lenin had different ideas from many of the other Bolshevik leaders, not to mention the population, about which direction the revolution should take. For Lenin, power rested with the proletariat, or working class. The Bolshevik party was its vanguard and therefore had the right to map out the route to socialism. The gulf between the aspirations of the working class, as expressed by party and non-party members alike, and the Bolshevik party leadership widened during the Civil War of 1918–20, and in 1921, a dismayed Lenin declared that the Russian working class 'had ceased to exist as a proletariat'.

Lenin never thought for a second that it was he and the Bolshevik leaders who were out of step with the working class. No, the majority was out of step with the minority. Since the Bolsheviks wished to remain in power, they were faced with two options: either adopt policies which found favour with the population, or substitute themselves for civil society. They chose the latter. In order to sustain themselves in power, they had to rely increasingly on the instruments of coercion, chiefly the political police, the Cheka, and to construct a bureaucracy which would channel the orders of the centre downwards and ensure that they were carried out. The egalitarian nature of the October Revolution disappeared very quickly as privileges, mainly in kind, began to reward those found loyal. The makings of a ruling class are discernible under Lenin. Classical Marxism abhors the state; it is an instrument of oppression. Lenin resurrected it in a new guise. The state *per se* was not bad, it was only bad if the levers of power were in capitalist hands. If the hands at the tiller were socialist, then it was a power for good in the land.

Under Stalin the state expanded mightily. Industrialisation, collectivisation and modernisation were administered from above. However the personal dictatorship of Stalin involved the destruction of all independent centres of social power. The purges, reaching their zenith in 1936–38, conflicted with the need to establish an effective bureaucratic and legal system to direct change from above.

After Stalin died in 1953, Khrushchev dispensed with mass terror as an instrument of rule. This, however, meant that Soviet leaders had to motivate and mobilise the population to carry out the political, economic and social goals enunciated by the communist party. As coercion dropped, so legitimacy – or the identification of the population with the goals of the leadership – had to rise. In other words, the gulf between the rulers and the ruled had to diminish. Khrushchev had a deep faith in the creative potential of the Soviet population and this populist streak led him into sharp conflict with the ruling bureaucracies. In his search for a more efficient system, he introduced many reforms and eventually alienated all the bureaucratic élites. His decision to split the party apparatus, his own power base, in 1962 was the last straw. From 1962–4 he set in motion changes which could have fundamentally altered the Soviet political system.

However, society was not able to grasp the opportunities offered, due to the lack of autonomous channels of communication and organisational experience. After Khrushchev's removal in October 1964, the party and state bureaucracies reasserted their authority. Brezhnev was faced with the modernisation of the Soviet Union, only partly achieved by Khrushchev, at a time when the United States was becoming increasingly involved in Vietnam. Whereas the debate about national security after Stalin's death had led to peaceful co-existence, that over the years 1965-7 saw the influence of the military mount. The diversion of increasing resources to the military sector led to an unprecedented arms build-up, and in 1969, the Soviet Union achieved parity with the United States in certain weapons systems.

By the mid-1970s, the Soviet Union felt strong enough to be increasingly self-assertive in foreign policy. By outmanoeuvring the Americans in Africa for example, the Soviet leadership could feel that it had achieved a long-standing goal of Russian and Soviet foreign policy – being on a par with, or even superior to, the West. Along with this policy went détente, which can be traced back to 1962, just as Khrushchev's policy of peaceful co-existence was accompanied by an arms build-up which resulted in the confrontation with the United States over Cuba in 1962.

The new military might of the Soviet Union has gone hand in hand with an increase in the influence of the military in foreign policy formation. Indeed, one of the characteristics of the Brezhnev era was the militarisation of society, as the party and the military stoked up the fires of patriotism and played on the population's fear of war. Mounting military might has been bought at a price. It has been estimated that 48 per cent of the output of the machine building industries is now earmarked for defence. If the defence sector is so privileged, the rest of the economy must suffer.

Brezhnev's careful, skilful political strategy consolidated his power and he learned from Khrushchev's mistakes. He sought to avoid alienating bureaucratic interests and élites. He was a man of compromise not of reform. The Brezhnev era saw the party and state bureaucracies come into their own.

Central to developments in the Soviet Union is the Communist Party of the Soviet Union (CPSU). With over 17 million members, it is the only political party permitted. Under Brezhnev it consolidated its primacy in decision making. Some would question whether the CPSU is a party since it is not strictly one in the Western sense of the word. Parties in the West are concerned about winning votes and provide alternative channels of communication and organisation for the population. Political strategies can be changed overnight if a ruling party loses power. The multi-party system is highly flexible in formulating and responding to the mood of the electors. The single party, on the other hand, is not geared to winning votes but to achieving goals. Since it has to represent everyone, it has taken over some functions normally associated with the concept of the state. But, wedded to the leading role of the working class, it has less room for manoeuvre when seeking to dispense with outmoded political maxims.

The party's main claim to legitimacy is that it embodies the 'general will' of the population. It has therefore the right to set goals and prepare the way to the distant goal of communism. Public opinion is a pluralist concept, originating in opposition to absolutist rule. As such there can be no legitimate public opinion in the Soviet Union since it would challenge the hegemony of the party and would lead to confusion about socialist goals. Also the tradition of the autonomous individual in Western pluralist thought has no place in Marxism–Leninism. The CPSU claims to speak for all Soviet citizens since it is in a unique position to appreciate the needs of the whole population. An individual can only see a part, the party sees the whole.

A key element in the party's appeal is that its policies have been politically, economically and socially successful. The Soviet Union is a superpower and a force in world affairs – clear evidence of the party's successful track record. Domestically, economic growth is regarded as vital. Here the party is in a quandary, since there is always a conflict between politics and economics. Lenin turned Marx on his head by insisting on the primacy of politics. In other words, maintaining party control is the first priority. This has led to a vast bureaucratic system, with the party attempting to manage a modern, increasingly technically complex society.

If the goal of the CPSU were an efficiently functioning, modern society, then the centrally planned economy would be dismantled. (It would be more correct to call the present Soviet economy centrally managed rather than centrally planned, since it is impossible to plan the activities of some 49,000 enterprises producing over four million different products from the centre.) Managers would have a major say in what the enterprise produced and this, in turn, would depend on customers' preferences. Prices would find their own level. In agriculture, the private sector would expand, especially in animal husbandry, and farms would be allowed to buy their own machinery and equipment direct from the factory. The centre's tasks would be to respond to the signals reaching it and to encapsulate them in its guidance of society. Autonomous institutions would be a necessary prerequisite for such a development. Technical competence would become the main criterion for obtaining a post, thus consigning the party's right to appoint whomever it pleases to oblivion.

Since the party asserts the primacy of politics, it arrogates the right to guide society. In other words, if society were left to develop spontaneously, it would choose false goals. Hence society, if given a choice, would not of its own volition choose communism – communism, that is, as defined by the party. Hence a goal of the party is to prevent the coalescence of sections of the population into interest groups articulating their autonomous aspirations. The party and state bureaucracies strive to avoid social influences penetrating to the centre of the decision-making process. Of course, they take such influences into account when making decisions, but on their own terms. There is considerable participation in the Soviet political process, but it usually takes the form of mobilisation and as such is mediated by the party. Socialisation, by definition, is a controlled process.

As the party expands it embraces all the key élites, and in so doing becomes more professional. However, the party is confronted by a dilemma. The administration and the management of the economy need more modern and rational methods. Yet opting for change could lead to the erosion of the party's leading role. This dilemma cannot be solved by the party ensuring that its members are the decision makers, since the loyalty of a computer specialist will primarily be to his discipline. As science and technology become more complex, so those Soviet leaders without the requisite background will feel more and more like fishes out of water.

The party performs important functions in the present bureaucratic system. It mediates interests and conflicts and is an early warning system for disaffection among the non-Russian nationalities. Were it not so powerful, the Soviet Union would become a series of regions pushing their own interests.

The emergence of dissent and opposition under Brezhnev may presage the evolution of a politically more sophisticated civil society. Higher standards of education and culture, allied to the fact that increasing urbanisation brings more people together, may give rise to autonomous lines of communication. In order to influence the decision makers at the centre, civil society would need to articulate its aspirations through institutions not dominated by the value system of the centre. This would necessarily be a slow process. On the other hand, mounting economic difficulties have led the party to lay greater stress on *partiinost* or party-mindedness since the mid-1970s.

It is clear that Andropov will start as part of a collective leadership. This was the case after Lenin, Stalin and Khrushchev passed from the political scene. The constraints of the Soviet political system have always led to the emergence of a national leader within a period of five years or more. The personality of the man who emerges has played a more significant part in the shaping of Soviet policies than in any other modern nation. Andropov is schooled and socialised by the party and state apparatuses; since his base is in the central bureaucracy, he will have to satisfy the demands of the bureaucratic élites. If life goes on as under Brezhnev, there will be little change internally or externally. However, if the economy continues to falter and the military becomes an increasing financial burden, the way will be open for a reformer. A crackdown on absenteeism, corruption, alcoholism, low labour productivity; an ending of job security; an increase in the price of bread, meat and other consumer products are all necessary if the Soviet system is to become more efficient. Such unpopular reforms could only be forced on the bureaucracies and the population if everyone believed that a major war was on the horizon. Hence the present policy of the Reagan administration could backfire and lead the Soviet leader to galvanise the nation to such an extent that the Soviet Union becomes a more formidable competitor.

On the other hand, a foreign policy crisis and a faltering economy could increase the role of the instruments of coercion, the military and the police. The Brezhnev era saw a slow but sure militarisation of society. This process is not unique to the USSR, it is also very perceptible in the German Democratic Republic. Given the need to retain party control, economic efficiency may again be sacrificed. This will lead to a situation in which the military sector of the economy continues to grow at the expense of the civilian sector. The military sector is often viewed as efficient, but this is misleading; it is a high priority sector, and as such secures its inputs at the expense of the rest of the economy. Since it recruits most of the best scientific and technical expertise, it is not surprising that agricultural engineering, for example, leaves much to be desired. Perhaps some American policy makers believe that if the Soviet Union is forced into a new arms race, it will lead to the military sector crippling the economy. The second priority area of the Soviet economy, agriculture, is very wasteful of resources. One can envisage a situation in the later 1980s when defence and agriculture could account for over half of annual investment. In this case, sectors such as health and housing – about which the average Soviet citizen has been most disappointed over the last decade – will lag far behind. Hence the external factors will have a considerable influence on the policies adopted by a new leadership.

Just how significant is dissent and opposition in the Soviet Union? Is it likely to grow during the 1980s? The demise of the Moscow Monitoring Group testifies to the efficiency of the political police (KGB) in eliminating overt manifestations of protest. All criticism of Soviet policy will increasingly have to be clandestinely conducted underground.

Iain Elliot sees discontent as widespread in Soviet society, but, given the power of the party and the police, it poses little threat to the regime at present. In the field of nationality policy, the KGB has been markedly successful in suppressing the more articulate proponents of Ukrainian separatism and those who oppose the onrushing tide of Russian culture. There is much *samizdat* (self-publishing) activity in Lithuania and Estonia, with the influence of the Roman Catholic Church being significant in Lithuania. National consciousness is also well developed in Armenia and Georgia. The Muslim republics present an unknown quantity. Muslims will in the near future make up 20 per cent of the Soviet population, and the annual population increase is now almost entirely Muslim. Little is known of their aspirations, since there is a paucity of Islamic *samizdat* material.

There are various groups with political platforms which favour a radical transformation of society, but so far their impact has been muted. One Soviet estimate of the predilections of the population is that five per cent are convinced supporters of the regime, five per cent are active opponents and the rest are apathetic. This ability to make politics boring and to convince all but a small minority that active opposition is futile can be seen as one of the great strengths of the Soviet regime. Given the astonishing stability of basic Soviet structures under Brezhnev, why should the regime devote such energy to silencing the small minority who oppose it? The communist party is mindful of its own progress from a small clandestine party to power in 1917. A tiny band of determined men and women *can* change the world.

Iain Elliot's conclusion is that support for the regime is passive rather than active, but that foreign adventures and a rapid dip in living standards could transform dissent into mass opposition.

Alan Smith discusses whether the Soviet economic system can survive without substantial reform. A key factor in resolving this problem is Soviet self-sufficiency in natural resources. The continued survival of the basically unreformed Stalinist economic system has depended on self-sufficiency. What if domestic demand for energy outgrows domestic supply? Natural gas is not a problem but oil is. The Soviet Union is already cutting back on oil exports to Eastern Europe, but natural gas deliveries may rise. Given the possible need of the Soviet Union to import oil, is it advisable for the West to help build the Siberian pipeline, which will bring vast quantities of natural gas to Western Europe? Besides oil, the USSR usually needs to import agricultural commodities and some high technology products annually. Alan Smith sees the current economic system surviving, but with a few changes in policy due to the Soviet ability to export gold, diamonds and arms to meet the cost of food imports. The USSR has shown a declining interest in importing Western technology since the mid-1970s. The picture changes, however, when one considers the Soviet Union's commitments in Eastern Europe, South East Asia, Afghanistan and Cuba. The cost of propping up these regimes is becoming increasingly burdensome.

Despite agriculture being a high priority sector of the economy, its present performance is disappointing. Alec Nove suggests that one of the reasons for this is the problem of planning. Farm hands need to use their initiative since it is very difficult to supervise the work process over such a wide area. Looking to Hungary will not really help. The abundance of food there is the result of a very flexible system which provides real incentives to farms and private producers to increase output. One of the factors in the Hungarian success story is the ability of the farms to buy their machinery and equipment direct from the factory. An industrial reform would be necessary in the Soviet Union before this system could be adopted. The goal of the Soviet leadership is self-sufficiency, but a major problem is the price of basic foodstuffs such as bread and meat; they are too cheap. The Polish example may serve as a warning to the new leadership not to meddle in such things, but unless prices are raised there is no way the Soviet Union can meet domestic demand.

Philip Hanson holds out little hope for increased East–West trade throughout the 1980s. Improved political relations are necessary before any substantial change in Soviet–Western trade can be expected. Nevertheless, Western trade is very attractive to Soviet policy makers.

Jonathan Alford does not accept the view that a military solution in either Western Europe or the Far East is sufficiently free of risk to warrant its adoption as a realistic policy option for the Soviet leadership. He sees little correlation between military build-up and external threat. The build-up appears to have developed its own momentum. There is little comfort to be derived from the view that the Soviets are wedded to overinsurance, since the line between offence and defence in Soviet thinking is hazy. Soviet military might is being increasingly used for political ends.

Turning to foreign policy, there are three main ways of analysing Soviet behaviour:

(i) ideological: goals are determined primarily by an expansionist ideology which sees confrontation – short of war, if at all possible – with capitalism as inevitable, and this state of affairs will last until the final victory of socialism on a world scale;
(ii) *Realpolitik*: the Soviet Union as a great power is concerned with expanding its influence throughout the world. Ideological formulations serve merely to add legitimacy to policy goals; and
(iii) opportunism: although the Soviet Union may have a grand design for world power – like any major state – it seeks to achieve this by seizing all the opportunities on offer to it. Hence it is essentially reactive, and is not a prime initiator of events.

Coming to terms with the USSR is much easier if (ii) and (iii) are adopted. In both cases a viable agreement or *modus vivendi* is feasible and possible. However, if (i) is taken as the basis of analysis, no meaningful agreement can be reached with the Kremlin.

George Schöpflin argues that the Soviet Union lacks a concept of alliance and only understands subordination. Hence Soviet–East

European relations are qualitatively different from the practice of international relations in other parts of the world. He sees the Soviet goal as the concentration of power at the centre in each East European state. There are two tiers of control in Eastern Europe, the Soviet and the local, with the latter appearing alien to the local population. This is acceptable to the Soviets since it increases the dependence of these élites on the Soviet Union. The military take-over in Poland has initiated a new era in communist politics. Eastern Europe will remain unstable until there is a qualitative change in the Soviet–East European relationship, allowing local political traditions to reassert themselves. George Schöpflin, however, sees little likelihood of this being tolerated by the new Soviet leadership. As before, the Soviets will prefer to pay the costs rather than permit fundamental change.

Turning to relations with China, the goal of Soviet policy is clear: to bring China back into the socialist commonwealth, with the Communist Party of China acknowledging the leading role of the CPSU. As Christina Holmes concludes, there has never been a Sino–Soviet friendship, since China has had much to complain about ever since 1949 and indeed the Chinese communist leadership was in conflict with Moscow long before that. When the Chinese discovered that aid meant trade to the Soviets, they realised that economic development would be long and arduous. The Soviets were certainly not going to favour the Chinese. There is little or no hope of party-to-party relations improving unless the Chinese back down ideologically, but state-to-state relations could improve.

Part of the problem is that Soviet negotiators, like their Russian predecessors, appear to face difficulties when dealing with some Asian powers. It is striking that throughout the 20th century relations with Japan and China have been almost uniformly bad. At present relations with the People's Democratic Republic of Korea leave much to be desired. Is there a subconscious racial bias at work? It may be that the inability of the Soviets to make concessions or admit mistakes is the key factor. If they give way on the Kurile islands, thereby improving relations with Japan, the Chinese will require comparable concessions or vice versa. If China wishes to modernise rapidly, it will need to sustain good relations with the West, especially the United States. The closer China moves to the West, the more alarmed the Soviet Union will become, thereby fuelling its fears of encirclement.

Many Americans have come to the conclusion that détente was a one-way street – all the concessions were made by the West, especially the United States, and all the gains accrued to the Soviet Union. A new term is needed to describe the present state of relations between the superpowers. Hugh Seton-Watson's conclusion is that détente is not dead since it has yet to be born. He views Soviet policy towards the

West as one of unrelenting hostility. In the competition between systems the Soviets are not willing to give an inch. Some Soviet citizens, notably Academician Andrei Sakharov, view the 'confrontation' as irrelevant in a world plagued by hunger, disease and pollution. In reality, such men have little or no chance of translating their views into policies since they do not possess political power and are most unlikely to acquire any. What the Politburo decides is of paramount importance, and it is in the fortunate position of being able to ignore Soviet public opinion when formulating foreign policy.

The Soviet Union during the Brezhnev era was remarkably stable. The strengths of the system, with the primacy of politics over economics and the party taking over the role of civil society, were far greater than the weaknesses. The search for a more modern and efficient mode of rule for an increasingly complex society could undermine that stability. One reason why moderate Stalinism is still evident is that it is an effective way of ruling the country. Western socialists and liberals have had their hopes for a genuine de-Stalinisation of the system dashed time and time again. Their hopes always rise when a new leader takes over. They look for the evolution of independent lines of communication and institutions, without which civil society cannot reclaim its power.

Andropov gives the impression of a man capable of incisive leadership. He is the best educated leader since Lenin and is well aware of the strengths and weaknesses of the Soviet Union – gleaned from his years as head of the KGB. The political police, unlike the party and state apparatuses, have no incentive to camouflage the reality of everyday problems. However, Andropov's first task will be to concentrate on strengthening his own position. If he is able to purge the Brezhnevites rapidly, he could become the national leader quite quickly. Then he will be in a position to attempt to solve the many problems left behind by the Brezhnev leadership. His ability to do this will depend on his influence over the bureaucracy. It will be easier to check on the implementation of instructions by the party bureaucracy than the much larger state bureaucracy.

Nevertheless, he faces the prospect that bureaucratic inertia will be able to vitiate his well-meaning administrative and economic reforms. Here his persuasive skills will be put to the test as he is quite aware that the bureaucrats defeated Khrushchev's attempts to cut down their power and privilege. Under Brezhnev, stability and consensus were the orders of the day and this means that the bureaucracy is now a formidable obstacle to change. Brezhnev promised several administrative reforms towards the end of his life, but none of them ever saw the light of day.

Andropov has the option of being flexible in foreign policy. Repairing fences with China is one of his priorities, but this has to be linked to a face-saving solution to the Afghan problem. His relations with the military are likely to become closer, with the marshals securing an ever-increasing slice of national investment. However, a new arms race and continuing agricultural failure could cripple the economy. This would reduce the party's ability to mediate political, economic and social conflicts. Lack of success at home might lead to an aggressive foreign policy, with the Soviet Union's military might being used to secure advantage abroad. The declining legitimacy of the party domestically would be countered by Soviet expansion abroad. However, the Soviet political system is conservative and is well aware of the unpredictable consequences of armed struggle. This is the message for the 1980s.

2 Leadership and the Succession Struggle
Martin McCauley

Introduction

There are four ways in which the Soviet Union can change its leader: the death of the incumbent; his incapacitation through illness; his resignation; or his enforced removal. Each has different political implications and each is quite possible. In the course of the USSR's existance since 1917, there have only been four undisputed leaders: Lenin, Stalin, Khrushchev and Brezhnev. This leaves out Malenkov, who was a key secretary of the Central Committee (CC) of the Communist Party of the Soviet Union (CPSU) for just a week after Stalin's death in March 1953 and was chairman of the USSR Council of Ministers for almost two years. Lenin, Stalin and Brezhnev died and Khrushchev fell victim to a successful coup.

It is now a commonplace that the Soviet leader occupies the post of Secretary General of the CPSU and that his main power base is the party apparatus. (Between 1952 and 1966 the party leader was called the First Secretary.) However before 1953 this was not the case. The first, and arguably the only leader with charisma, Vladimir Ilich Lenin, was not even a secretary of the communist party. His main office was that of chairman of the Council of People's Commissars (Sovnarkom), the post he preferred since he was enamoured of administration. Of course he was a member of the highest party organ, the CC (1917–19), and then the Politburo, but his power and authority did not derive from any office, it was based on his intellectual dominance and the fact that he had led the Bolsheviks to victory in October 1917. Although his cabinet was Sovnarkom, members could appeal over his head to the Politburo. Hence, when he suffered his first stroke in 1922, it was not clear which institution was stronger. However he was disturbed by the Politburo's accumulation of responsibilities, many of which he regarded as the legitimate tasks of government. Undoubtedly, he would have reversed this trend had he been physically able to do so.

When Lenin died it was not clear whether the head of government was the new leader. A collective leadership came into being until Stalin was able to achieve primacy by 1929. He was Secretary General of the CPSU between 1922 and 1934 and afterwards a secretary until his death. He was also Prime Minister between 1941 and 1953. The basis of his power initially was the party apparatus, which is composed of full-time, paid officials. Control of the political police, now called the KGB, during the 1930s allowed him to crush opposition in the party and government bureaucracies. The military, the only other institution which posed a possible threat to his power, was cruelly decimated during the 1930s.

Again, on Stalin's death, it was unclear whether the leader of the country would be the head of the government or the party leader, since Stalin had subordinated both to his own autocratic rule. Stalin ruled through a 'special department' he set up for the task. Collective leadership reappeared until Khrushchev, using the party as his base, gradually overcame Malenkov and then his opponents in the Politburo. When Khrushchev was removed, a new collective leadership took over, consisting of L.I. Brezhnev, the new party leader, A.I. Kosygin, the Prime Minister, and N.V. Podgorny, the chairman of the presidium of the USSR Supreme Soviet – the Soviet President. Brezhnev, as head of the party, occupied the senior position. By 1969 he had become the national leader, although the semblance of a collective leadership was maintained. Brezhnev, in turn, has been succeeded by a collective leadership with the Secretary General the senior figure. (See pages 37–9 for details of the present Soviet leadership.)

The succession

Although there have been only three successions, a pattern does emerge. Each new party leader has inherited less power over policy than his predecessor, but has managed, during his term of office, to increase his power and to become clearly identifiable as the national leader. Toward the end of his office the leader noticeably loses some of his ability to force through his policies. This happened to Lenin, Stalin, Khrushchev and Brezhnev in turn. The periods of collective leadership are those during which there is a succession struggle (between 1922 and 1929, 1953 and 1957, and 1964 and 1969), otherwise a particular leader is clearly *primus inter pares*. The years between 1934 and 1953 (to a lesser extent during the war years), when Stalin held the power of life or death over his colleagues, are an exception and unlikely to recur.

Two styles of leadership are evident. Lenin, Stalin and Khrushchev led from the front but Brezhnev led from the middle. The former style entails great risks, since policy failure can lead to a drop in authority and the risk of removal. Lenin threatened on more than one occasion during the first year of the revolution to resign unless his advice was taken, but his personal authority ensured success for his proposals. (Had he been outvoted, he would have left the CC and carried on in opposition until he had won over a majority of the CC to his way of thinking. It is unfortunate that this state of affairs never came about since it would have established a valuable precedent.)

Even though Stalin was *primus inter pares* he was restricted in his policy initiatives until 1934, but afterwards he employed coercion against his opponents.

Khrushchev, after 1954, abjured the use of violence and bloodletting against political foes. This involved trying to forge a consensus in the party and government bureaucracies for his policies. His task was made all the more difficult in that he was, like Lenin and Stalin, a 'revolutionary' leader. He was innovative, dynamic and always full of ideas on how to advance the Soviet Union towards communism. Since a 'revolutionary' leader is bound to be disappointed with his achievements – Lenin certainly was and Stalin failed to achieve many of his goals – he is inclined to develop 'reform mania'. This was Khrushchev's undoing. By 1964 he had antagonised so many bureaucratic interests that his authority had sunk to a very low level. Brezhnev, on the other hand, never made this mistake.

The different levels of power that the Soviet Union's leaders have exercised stem from the lack of a legal or constitutional definition of the rights and duties of the chief executive. The CPSU does not mention in its statutes the position of leader, merely that of the Secretary General (Article 38). The top party official in a republic, oblast (subdivision of republic) or city is called the First Secretary, but this title does not appear in the statutes. Incidentally there is no reason why the Prime Minister should not become the leader since he is always a member of the Politburo. However Article 6 of the 1977 constitution calls the party the 'leading and guiding force of Soviet society' as Marxism–Leninism, the ruling ideology, is the fountain of systemic legitimacy. Thus the Soviet Union lacks any provision for political succession. There is no mechanism for a long-term sharing or transfer of leadership at the top, and the leading role of the party is exercised without any formal procedure for consultation with social forces or government ministries (Rakowska-Harmstone, 1976: 52).

It follows that the Secretary General, the party leader, stands the best chance of becoming the national leader. In the latter role, however, he is required to resolve conflicts in all policy areas and to be able to demonstrate that the country, under his guidance, is a success both domestically and in foreign policy. In short, he has to acquire personal, as well as systemic, legitimacy, a command over the instruments of power and be able to claim that his policies have been crowned with success.

In a pluralist society, periodic elections confer on the party in power its legitimacy, but in a one-party state such as the USSR, this is replaced by the ideology, which claims to be the infallible guide to a richer and better life. The leader personifies this ideology and, since it has to keep in step with life, which is dynamic, he is responsible for reformulating it from time to time. The leading role of the communist party precludes any other source of political power, but the doctrine of democratic centralism in all institutions means that there are many conflicting bureaucracies at the centre over which the leader must gain dominance. If there is a clear leader, he can manipulate these bureaucracies for his own ends, but during a collective leadership competing interests emerge which tend to balance one another. This state of affairs could last indefinitely but it would not produce any viable solutions to pressing problems and would probably lead to a crisis. The demands of the party and state bureaucracies, the political police, the military and social groups, such as the intelligentsia and workers, cannot be ignored for ever.

Legitimacy
The Soviet political system has developed quite a high level of legitimacy during its years in power. The charismatic Lenin seemed to many to be the new 'tsar', a natural leader for the new state. He adopted many of the traditional Russian methods of rule. Concentration of power at the centre, an all-embracing bureaucracy, the rights of the state taking precedence over those of the individual and a pervasive political police. It is true that he was disappointed that traditional values and ways of doing things were so deep, but he had little time to change them fundamentally. Stalin attempted to cultivate a charisma – a contradiction in terms – and projected himself as omniscient and indispensable and the embodiment of society. He was the *vozhd* or Führer of his people. He was also their father but remained rather aloof from his children. Khrushchev was ebullient and folksy but too common for general taste. The Soviets prefer their leaders to be distant, serious and aware of tradition. Brezhnev paid particular attention to these aspects. When leaders emerge they foster a cult of the personality: in Lenin's case he resisted this, but the others consciously luxuriated in it. An important element in such a cult is the ability to pronounce on ideology. Lenin was very creative in this respect. Stalin projected the view, among others, that class struggle intensifies as the Soviet Union approaches socialism; Khrushchev introduced the all people's state; and Brezhnev promulgated developed socialism. Leaders often award themselves medals and prizes to underline their success and Brezhnev had several Hero of the Soviet Union and Order of Lenin medals. He also received the Lenin Peace Prize in 1973, became a Marshal of the Soviet Union in 1976 and received the Order of Victory, the highest military award, in 1978. The Lenin Prize for Literature (for his memoirs) came his way in 1979; the Brezhnev cult of the personality increased as he physically declined.

The top posts in the Soviet Union are the heads of the party, government and the state. Both Stalin and Khrushchev were heads of the party and the government, but when the latter was removed in 1964, it was agreed that no single person should hold both offices simultaneously. However this did not prevent Brezhnev from conducting important foreign policy negotiations from the late 1960s onwards or from signing the Helsinki Final Act in 1975, a sure guide to his increased power. Since he could not head the government, he set out to downgrade it and in 1977 he became president. Article 6 of the 1977 constitution states that the party is the leading and guiding force in the country and, as such, the Prime Minister is subject to the party leader. Also Article 130 states that the USSR Council of Ministers is responsible to the USSR Supreme Soviet and, when it is not in session, to the presidium of the USSR Supreme Soviet. As President Brezhnev was chairman of this presidium.

The instruments of power

It is essential for an aspiring leader moving up to cultivate the support of the key central bureaucracies and, when in power, to satisfy them. Stalin was very successful in this regard but Khrushchev was an abject failure. Since there are no institutional means for bringing different groups of the population and their aspirations into contact with decision makers, they have to be channelled through the bureaucracy. The final arbiter is the party and it performs a function akin to the market in a pluralist society. During times of collective leadership, leading figures speak for their 'interest groups' and in so doing attempt to discredit the claims of others. A popular technique is to label competing claims un-Leninist or revisionist, even though the argument may for example, be about how to increase the efficiency of the planning system.

Control of the apparatus is absolutely essential to a leader. He has at his disposal an army of about 300,000 paid, full-time officials. The party embraces more than 17 million members in a population of over 270 millions. This apparatus is the instrument for implementing the leading role of the party and three devices are used to achieve this. By means of the *nomenklatura*, which is both a list of appointments which require party approval and and a list of the names of those persons suitable for the relevant post, it can place its own members in all key positions in state and society. It also co-opts specialists and other élite figures to serve on its own executive committees. For instance, a city committee may include engineers, doctors and artists. All executive organs of state and government have a parallel party organ. The party cell, the primary party organisation, is also constitutionally the core of all organisations and institutions. Hence, besides the Soviet government there is a parallel government, the communist party apparatus, whose task is to supervise, control and guide all other institutions. A key objective of party organs is to ensure that party directives are implemented in the economy and society.

The government bureaucracy is much larger than the party bureaucracy and has all-Union and Union-republican ministries. The former embrace the whole of the Soviet Union, while the latter only function within the relevant republic. Democratic centralism is the guiding principle of government as well as the party but given the mammoth tasks involved, the government bureaucracy is more prone to 'localism'. Since party officials are held responsible for the economic success of their area, they become closely involved and often allocate resources. The primacy placed on heavy industry means that these ministries and the main centres of production have considerable political influence and this adds to the prestige of the relevant party officials. The road to the top is paved with economic success, first and foremost in heavy industry.

The allocation of resources is of key importance. Party and state organs unite in an attempt to obtain more investment and goods for 'their' republic, oblast or city. An official in Krasnodar krai, a fertile agricultural region in the North Caucasus told me that when his delegation went to Moscow 'they went armed for war'. He meant that Moscow automatically assumed that Krasnodar was trying to pull the wool over their eyes and the more convincingly they put their case, the more resources they received. This underlines the fact that the provinces 'gang up' against the centre. Cities in the Soviet Union are graded. First comes Moscow, then Leningrad, then Kiev and then the others. The higher up in the pecking order, the more political weight the party secretary carries.

The political police and the military, the instruments of coercion, are of primary importance in maintaining the power of the leader and the communist party. They control the armed troops and play important, even decisive, roles during periods of crisis. This can be illustrated by some aspects of the succession struggle which occurred after Stalin's death. The political police were then very strong and their head, Lavrenty Beria, was a candidate for national leadership. Malenkov, seen by many as the heir apparent in March 1953, had become Prime Minister and a secretary of the CC. However, since Malenkov's opponents had been able to abolish the post of Secretary General of the party at the 19th Party Congress in October 1952, Malenkov could not occupy the top party post after Stalin's death since no such post, strictly speaking, existed.

However Malenkov only remained party secretary a week. As Prime Minister, he entered into a tactical alliance with Beria. The other power base, the party, gradually came under Khrushchev's control. Since Malenkov could no longer use the resources of the CPSU secretariat, he began to establish parallel organs in the government bureaucracy. Khrushchev managed to drive a wedge between Malenkov and Beria and the latter fell in June 1953. Various rumours circulated to the effect that Beria had attempted a coup and had employed his own troops, but that the military had remained loyal to the party and the government. Beria's fall removed the political police as a barrier to party supremacy. Then it became a straight contest between the party and the government, or between Khrushchev and Malenkov.

The latter resigned in February 1955, and Khrushchev attempted to undermine the government bureaucracy by decentralising economic decision making in 1957. In so doing he abolished the economic ministries and the government representatives in the Politburo reacted strongly in defence of their power bases and attempted to dismiss Khrushchev as party leader. They failed and were labelled the 'anti-party group'. Although they had a majority in the Politburo, they allowed a CC plenum to convene, during which Khrushchev's supporters carried the day. Both the political police and the military sided with Khrushchev and made an important contribution to his victory. The 'anti-party group' planned to remove General Ivan Serov as head of the KGB to gain access to the archives. The KGB and the military put their resources at Khrushchev's disposal and the latter's supporters were ferried to the Kremlin in time. Afterwards, Marshal Georgy Zhukov was made a full member of the Politburo and USSR Minister of Defence.

Brezhnev's rise to power

A sure way of judging why a leader is removed is to examine changes afterwards. The bifurcation of the party into industrial and non-industrial wings, adopted by Khrushchev in 1962 in an attempt to make it a more pliant executor of his policy decisions, was quickly ended after his fall, and the regional bureaux dissolved, except for the RSFSR bureau. It survived two years, possibly because Brezhnev was trying to use it to build up a personal power base (Rakowska-Harmstone 1976: 61). Restrictions on tenure and turnover provisions were scrapped. Khrushchev had clearly riled the top party bureaucrats. The councils of the national economy disappeared as the central economic ministries reappeared in Moscow in September 1965. This strengthened the institutional base of A.I. Kosygin, the Prime Minister.

Brezhnev's first priority was to increase his standing in the secretariat. At the December 1965 CC plenum, N.V. Podgorny, who had become a secretary after Khrushchev's removal, lost his position and became chairman of the presidium of the USSR Supreme Soviet, or

President. Since he remained in the Politburo, he was able to invest his new office with more authority. Another major competitor, A.N. Shelepin, lost the chairmanship of the Party-State Control Commission when it was abolished and the post of deputy chairman of the USSR Council of Ministers, all in 1965. Then in 1967 he was made chairman of the All-Union Central Council of Trade Unions. Since this post could not be held by a CC secretary he lost this position as well. As these men left the secretariat, Brezhnev could replace them with his own appointments. A.P. Kirilenko became secretary for cadres and he was elected to the Politburo in October 1964. He could then set about the task of building up a solid phalanx of 'Brezhnev men' round the country. Other secretaries appointed were Yuri Andropov, Rudakov and Titov. I.V. Kapitonov became a secretary in December 1965, as did S.M. Solomentsev in January 1966.

Brezhnev's position was strengthened after the 24th Party Congress in 1971 when P.E. Shelest, First Secretary in the Ukraine, and G.I. Voronov left the Politburo. In early 1973 D.S. Polyansky was made USSR Minister of Agriculture and lost his position as first deputy Prime Minister. Polyansky stayed in the Politburo, but, as USSR Minister of Agriculture, he was unlikely to be an economic success. These changes reflected the continued rise of Brezhnev and the decline of his two main rivals, Kosygin and Podgorny.

The promotion of Yuri Andropov, head of the KGB, Marshal Andrei Grechko, USSR Minister of Defence and Andrei Gromyko, USSR Minister of Foreign Affairs, to full membership of the Politburo in April 1973 increased the representation of functional élites there. It also balanced the influence of the party apparatus and made it less likely that a move against Brezhnev's position would succeed. The Secretary General had always cultivated the KGB and his contacts with the military went back to wartime days when he had been a political commissar.

Shelepin finally left the Politburo in April 1975, and four months later Brezhnev signed, on behalf of the Soviet Union, the Helsinki Final Act which saw the Western Powers acknowledge the post-war division of Europe. Détente, closely associated with the Secretary General, was bearing tangible fruit. At the 25th Party Congress, in March 1976, Brezhnev's position was further enhanced as G.V. Romanov, First Secretary of Leningrad oblast party organisation and D.F. Ustinov, CC secretary for defence, were promoted to full membership. Konstantin Chernenko and Mikhail Zimyanin became CC secretaries. In October 1977, Chernenko was promoted to candidate member (one who can attend and speak, but not vote) of the Politburo and in November 1978, became a full member – a meteoric rise. When Grechko died in April 1976, he was replaced as USSR Minister of Defence, not by a professional soldier but by a civilian, Ustinov. In 1977 Brezhnev became president, and Podgorny left the Politburo. In November 1978, Nikolai Tikhonov, Kosygin's deputy, became a candidate member of the Politburo and, a year later, a full member. He was made Prime Minister when Kosygin resigned, but clearly had less authority than his predecessor. Another functionary who also experienced a rapid rise to the top was Mikhail Gorbachev, who became CC secretary for agriculture in November 1978, a candidate member of the Politburo a year later and a full member in October 1980. The death of Mikhail Suslov, the party's leading ideologist, in January 1982, removed a formidable figure.

In May 1982, Yuri Andropov moved from his post as chairman of the KGB to 'other duties' in the Secretariat and V.I. Dolgikh became a candidate member of the Politburo.

When Brezhnev died in November 1982 the overwhelming majority of full and candidate members of the Politburo and the Secretariat were Brezhnev appointments. All his main competitors had passed from the scene. He had been careful not to allow an heir apparent to emerge and indeed some of the younger men who left the Politburo in the 1970s may have been too aggressive in pushing their own policies. Brezhnev preferred those of his own generation. Tikhonov, the present Prime Minister, was born in 1905 and his first deputy I.V. Arkhipov in 1907.

The key political institutions

The Politburo heads the list but its size has fluctuated over time. From a low of nine full and seven candidate members in July 1953, it rose to 16 full and seven candidate members in April 1973. It declined in size during the late 1970s, and on Brezhnev's death, contained 12 full and nine candidate members. The representation of the various bureaucracies has changed over time. In November 1982, besides the Secretary General, there were four other CC secretaries who were full members and two others candidate members; the chairman of the Party Control Commission had been a full member since 1957; the First Secretary of the CP of the Ukraine had been a full member since 1964; his counterpart in Kazakhstan a full member since 1971; the First Secretary in Uzbekistan a candidate member since 1961; his counterpart in Belorussia since 1966; the First Secretary in Azerbaidzhan since 1976; the First Secretary of the Moscow city party a full member since 1971, and his counterpart in the Leningrad oblast organisation since 1976. The chairman of the presidium of the USSR Supreme Soviet, the President, has always been a full member, as has the USSR Prime Minister.

Between 1953 and 1979 (except for the periods May–July 1957 and March 1963–March 1965), the first deputy Prime Minister had always been either a full or a candidate member, but the last holder of the office under Brezhnev, I.V. Arkhipov, was not even made a candidate member. The head of the KGB was a full member between 1973 and 1982. The USSR Minister of Defence and the USSR Minister of Foreign Affairs had been full members since 1973. The USSR Minister of Culture had been a candidate member since 1974, as had the Prime Minister of the RSFSR, since 1971. The chairman of the All-Union Central Council of Trade Unions was either a candidate or a full member between 1961 and Shelepin's removal in 1975. Hence of the 12 full members, four were CC secretaries, one was chairman of the Party Control Commission and besides the Prime Minister there were two other ministers. Until 1957 government representatives easily outnumbered party representatives, but since then the latter have dominated. However the disparity between the two bureaucracies was never so great as in 1982. Among candidate members, six of the nine were party functionaries, one was deputy President of the USSR, one the USSR Minister of Culture and the other the Prime Minister of the RSFSR.

Second only in importance to the Politburo as an institution is the Secretariat. If the Politburo is the Soviet cabinet, then the Politburo and the Secretariat together act as a parallel government. The Secretariat also prepares the materials which the Politburo uses in reaching decisions. It is responsible too for the implementation of Politburo decisions. Its head, the Secretary General, is the chairman of the Politburo and when he is absent, his place is taken by the second secretary; if the latter is away, the third secretary presides. Since the October 1980 CC plenum, the significance of the CC secretaries (each is responsible for a group of departments) in the leadership has increased. The number of departments in the Secretariat has increased from 21 to 24 since the 25th Party Congress in 1976. The new departments are: agricultural machine building; international information; and letters. The international information department is headed by Leonid Zamyatin and its task is to disseminate information about Soviet foreign policy more rapidly, inside and outside the party. The letters department is responsible for all correspondence received from ordinary people, in other words, a complaints commission. This department also has under its wing a Group for Analysing Public Opinion, Social Research and Development.

The third most important institution is the presidium of the USSR Council of Ministers, and in November 1982, it contained 14 men. Like the Politburo, it has a number of standing commissions, such as those on the defence industry, consumer goods industries and the Council for Mutual Economic Assistance (CMEA). It is quite possible that the Politburo commissions cover the same ground. The presidium acts as an economic cabinet and probably has joint sessions with the Politburo when particularly difficult economic problems are being discussed. The next institution in order of importance is the CPSU Central Committee. The CC elected at the 26th Party Congress in February–March 1981 contained 319 full and 151 candidate members, the largest ever. Representation of the various institutions is a guide to their relative standing. About three-quarters of the full members were re-elected, thus continuing a trend of the Brezhnev era, stability of cadres. The proportion of party officials rose slightly to 45 per cent. Of special interest is the rise of the CC apparatus, which is distinct from the CC Secretariat and includes the Party Control Commission and the Secretary General's personal staff. It now has 18 full members compared to five before the congress. A small decline in the proportion of republican and oblast party officials was also discernible, revealing a slight centralist trend. This was paralleled by a significant rise in the proportion of the representatives of the central state organs. The KGB and the military made some gains. The proportion of trade unionists, workers and peasants rose.

Since the CC is a useful barometer for the relative standing of the various bureaucracies and functional groups in the Soviet population, it is of some interest that about 83 per cent of the full members are party and government officials, about half in the party and half in the government bureaucracy. Another 8 per cent consist of top military and KGB officials. Hence top bureaucrats make up 91 per cent of the CC. The other 9 per cent is composed of members of the intelligentsia (not holding political–administrative posts), workers and collective farm peasants. Thus the CC overwhelmingly represents the interests of the various bureaucracies (Meissner, 1981: 14–15).

Between 1971 and 1976, the Politburo met on average almost once a week but more often than the Secretariat. Between 1976 and 1981 the Politburo met on 237 occasions, but the Secretariat convened on 250 occasions. Both met more often in 1976–81 than during the previous five-year period. On the other hand, the CC only met on 11 occasions and then only for a few days each, between 1976 and 1981. This is a far cry from the days under Stalin when these institutions scarcely met, and Khrushchev, in the early 1960s, was wont to make policy and then send a memorandum to the Politburo.

Policy making

There are three main areas in which a potential leader must be able to demonstrate policy success and meet the aspirations of social groups and nationalities. These are the economy, social problems and foreign policy. The declining real growth rate of the Soviet economy in the 1970s and early 1980s, especially the poor harvests, has concentrated minds on increasing efficiency. However without a rational pricing system the economy has to be guided to achieve set goals. Enterprises could, if given more autonomy, achieve more but this would diminish party control. The objective needs of the economy and party control clash, and so far the party has always won the day. It is worth noting that economic innovators have always lost in the struggle for power. During the 1920s, the left and the right were superbly played off against one another by Stalin, who appeared to represent the circumspect, middle of the road approach. Malenkov's 'New Course', with its emphasis on consumer goods at the expense of heavy industry and defence, was defeated by Khrushchev, who adopted an orthodox Stalinist approach. It is not sufficient for a potential leader to be conservative in economic policy, he has to offer solutions as well. Stalin's way out was rapid industrialisation and forced collectivisation. Khrushchev launched the 'Virgin Lands' programme and promised a rapid rise in food production. Once the leader is in the saddle he can, of course, adopt the policies of his defeated rivals. Stalin took the economic policies of the left and pushed them to excess and Khrushchev took over most of Malenkov's ideas. Kosygin's attempts to reform the industrial economy were frustrated. The entrenched interests of the economic bureaucracy and the plant managers resist radical change. This opens up possibilities for a potential leader who will defend their interests.

Social problems are rooted in the gulf between aspirations and reality. Intellectuals and the nationalities, for instance, want more autonomy but the party can only make token concessions. The experience of Eastern Europe, most notably Poland and Czechoslovakia, demonstrates the real danger which arises when the party makes concessions and the revolution of rising expectations is set in train. Stricter control is the only answer but this only postpones the next explosion of frustration and optimism. Much of this tension can be syphoned off by raising living standards.

The two facets of foreign policy – state interests and the revolutionary goals of the party – make it an important area of policy. The leader must adopt a policy which enhances the stature of the Soviet Union in the world at large, while aiding the struggle for socialism throughout the world as well. Devising a symbiotic relationship between the two inevitably leads to controversy. The rise of fascism, the cold war, the confrontation with China, the arms race and the conflict with the United States have profoundly affected the evolution of the USSR and foreign policy today, since it is so closely bound up with military might, occupies much of a leader's time.

If ill-thought-out experimentation was the hallmark of much of Khrushchev's economic and foreign policy, his successors have carefully avoided repeating his errors. No major economic reform has been instituted since 1964; the modest attempts in that direction have all run into the sand. In foreign policy, Brezhnev spawned détente and gave his name to the doctrine which in effect means that the Soviet state and party interests take precedence over those of other socialist states.

Brezhnev remained in power for so long by astute manœuvring in the party apparatus; by gradually whittling away the threat from the government bureaucracy; by allowing the power of the KGB and military to grow but under party surveillance; by avoiding any confrontations with the economic élites; by avoiding experimentation; and by expanding the influence of the USSR throughout the world. Konstantin Chernenko has summed up his style as the creation of a kind of 'moral and political atmosphere in the party and Soviet society in which as comrade L.I. Brezhnev says, "people breathe easily, work well and live tranquilly" ' (Chernenko 1978: 6). Brezhnev implied to Zdeněk Mlynář, who as a member of the Secretariat of the Communist Party of Czechoslovakia was shipped off to Moscow in the wake of the Warsaw Pact invasion in August 1968, that he was a reluctant invader and that, had he not joined the majority, he would have lost his position as party leader. He told another leading Czech communist that he only succeeded in getting about one-third of his proposals accepted by his colleagues in the Politburo (Brown 1980: 148).

Brezhnev's pragmatic, conservative leadership style, which came down to preserving his own position at all costs had, inevitably, its drawbacks: a declining industrial and agricultural performance; growing social problems, such as alcoholism; a lack-lustre ideology; and no foreseeable improvement in relations with China. As his health declined in the late 1970s, the jokes about him became more cruel. Afterwards the country drifted internally, with Brezhnev castigating government ministries, youth, workers and collective farm peasants but with little result. He bequeathed these and other headaches to his successors.

How to organise a coup
The most dangerous time for a leading politician is when he is out of the capital or abroad; long absences are inadvisable. One of the reasons for this is that the victim's supporters in the party and government apparatuses are at a disadvantage when trying to organise his defence. Khrushchev had been in Finland just before the 'anti-Party group' struck in June 1957; Zhukov was summoned to the Kremlin and informed on arrival home from an official visit to Yugoslavia and Albania in October 1957, that he had been dropped from the Politburo and relieved of his duties as USSR Minister of Defence; Shelepin was dismissed soon after returning from an unsuccessful visit to Britain in

April 1975; Podgorny lost the presidency and his seat in the Politburo in May 1977, about a month after returning from an extended African tour. When Khrushchev was removed in October 1964, he was enjoying the sunshine on the Black Sea shores instead of minding the shop in Moscow. Since it is the only successful coup instigated against a ruling leader, it is instructive in itself. It was masterminded by the KGB's former head, Aleksandr Shelepin, and the then head, Vladimir Semichastny. They isolated Khrushchev from his apparatus so he could not be informed of what was afoot. The fact that Khrushchev was far away on the Black Sea coast was significant; had he been at a *dacha* near Moscow, his supporters could have converged on the place by car. As the KGB has a parallel communications network, it did not need to use traditional channels. The KGB also provided the transport which brought the First Secretary to Moscow to face the Politburo. Had the military been on Khrushchev's side it might have saved him through its own communications network, aircraft and armed men. Since it was a coup, presumably only a minority of the Politburo participated in its planning. The question arises why Shelepin and Semichastny, both of whom lost their positions of power under Brezhnev, should have aided him to become party leader. It would appear that, in order to secure his wholehearted co-operation, Shelepin was led to believe that he might become the new party leader (Voslensky, 1980: 377).

The struggle for the succession

A striking factor about the Brezhnev era was the increase in the influence of the military and the concomitant militarisation of society. This made the military a powerful lobby for greater defence spending and in Brezhnev's declining years they needed to articulate their case with vigour and to find a successor who would see the world from their point of view. In order to give weight to their claim for increased defence spending, the military tend to paint the international scene in the blackest possible colours.

These views are forcefully articulated by Marshal Nikolai Ogarkov, chief of the General Staff and first deputy Minister of Defence. In an article entitled 'Defending Peaceful Labour' in the party theoretical journal *Kommunist* (no. 10/1981: 80–91) he made clear, by quoting Brezhnev, that the Soviet Union's strategic doctrines were 'of a fundamentally defensive character'. But should the enemy attack, the USSR was 'capable of launching an offensive operation on land, air and sea'. However, Ogarkov was far from happy about the attitude of many Soviet citizens:

The question of the struggle for peace is sometimes not understood from a class point of view but somewhat more simply: any peace is good, any war is bad.

This may lead to carelessness, complacency and apathy and to an under-rating of the danger of a possible war which in present circumstances would have serious consequences . . . in clarifying the complex nature of the international situation, it is necessary to bring home more clearly to Soviet citizens the truth about the present threat of war.

In order to awaken the public to the real state of affairs, Ogarkov advocated that the party intensify political and educational work among Soviet citizens. By painting the international scene in such dark colours, the chief of the General Staff was implicitly asking for greater defence spending. He pointed out that weapons systems change every 10–12 years and this meant that 'holdups in the development' of new methods of 'deploying the armed forces in wartime' were fraught with 'serious consequences'. The industrial economy had to be capable of replacing, in a short period of time, 'large quantities of combat hardware and weapons without which it is virtually impossible to maintain the combat capability of the armed forces at the required level'. He conceded that keeping the country on a war footing in peacetime was impractical but did not add that it would be prohibitively expensive.

Ogarkov's strongly worded article may have been a direct response to a speech by Konstantin Chernenko delivered on the occasion of the 111th anniversary of the birth of Vladimir Ilich Lenin (*Pravda* 23 April 1981). The CC Secretary was in a sombre mood and made the point that 'any nuclear confrontation would result in mankind suffering incalculable miseries'. He believed that it was 'criminal to regard nuclear war as a rational, almost "natural" extension of politics'. Responsible politicians were obliged to recognise that the use of nuclear weapons would 'place the future of mankind in doubt'. He went on to claim: 'The activities of some politicians on both sides of the Atlantic lead one to assume that they do not or will not comprehend this'. The concept of the 'limited' nuclear war was nothing less than an attempt to get people to accept a limited nuclear exchange. 'Comrades, this is why it is so important that the truth about the destructive consequences of a thermo-nuclear conflict be fully grasped by all peoples.' Chernenko was making clear his and, by extension, Brezhnev's view that a nuclear war could not be won. In this regard, his thoughts were reminiscent of those of Georgi Malenkov who articulated the doctrine of peaceful co-existence in 1953.

It transpired that Chernenko was out of step with some of his colleagues. The military lobby, represented in the Politburo by Dmitri Ustinov, USSR Minister of Defence, eventually won the day. At a meeting of top military personnel in the Kremlin on 27 October 1982, Leonid Brezhnev told his audience:

We equip the armed forces with the most advanced weapons and military matériel. The Party CC takes measures to ensure that you want for nothing.

And the armed forces should always be worthy of this concern. The time is now opportune that the combat readiness of the army and navy should be even higher. It is necessary to perfect combat readiness in a more responsible manner, proceeding from increasing requirements. Then nothing will take us unawares.

(*Pravda*, 28 October 1982)

On Soviet television the same evening, Ustinov commended Brezhnev for his 'political wisdom, restraint, firmness, courage and perspicacity'. He assured the Secretary General, who was also chairman of the Defence Council and a Marshal of the Soviet Union, that the 'elevation of the Soviet armed forces to a qualitatively new level of development and the steady increase in their combat strength and readiness' were linked with his name. At the Red Square parade on 7 November to mark the 65th anniversary of the Revolution, Ustinov continued:

The Soviet people and their army, for whom the defence of the socialist fatherland is near and dear to their heart, are invincible. Selflessly devoted to the socialist homeland, Soviet soldiers, in a united combat formation with the soldiers of the Warsaw Treaty states, are always ready to carry out with honour their patriotic and internationalist duty.

(*Pravda*, 8 November 1982)

If the military are concerned at the failure of some young Soviet people to take the threat of 'international imperialism' seriously, the KGB is alarmed at the inroads which Western life-styles and attitudes are making in the USSR. Viktor Chebrikov, a deputy chairman of the KGB, painted a picture of political cynicism and spiritual malaise among some Soviet youth in a youth journal (*Molodoi Kommunist* 4/1981: 28–34). He accused the West of using religion, nationalism and subversive political ideas to undermine the trust of young Soviet people in their communist party. Bourgeois ideology sought to 'create among some young people a feeling of apoliticism and nihilism' and encouraged them to 'adopt an anti-social attitude'. There was a widespread belief that life was better in the West. Foreign intelligence services were trying to convince young people that political pluralism was necessary in the Soviet Union to overcome the 'objective difficulties' which arise in social development. The conservatism of old cadres was preventing the 'democratisation and liberalisation of socialism' without which pressing problems could not be solved, it was claimed. He suggested that Ukrainian, Latvian, Armenian and Jewish émigré organisations were exerting considerable influence within the Soviet Union and were encouraging 'nationalist prejudices' and 'anti-social activities'.

(It is worth noting that Chebrikov himself has been subject to Western influence. His article is full of anglicisms, even using *'negativnye'* instead of the more usual *'otritsatelnye'* to convey the word 'negative'. This neatly illustrates the dilemma facing the Soviet leadership. They wish to demolish the common Soviet view that life is better in the West and to frighten the population into believing that 'Western imperialism' is threatening the very life of every Soviet citizen, while at the same time adopting more and more anglicisms. So fashionable have anglicisms become that even the KGB cannot resist the temptation to use them.)

The KGB is concerned about the fact that pop music is now replacing poetry as the mode of expression of the young. The best rock groups have English names and sing in English – often incomprehensible to singers and audience alike. Soviet pop music became a target, and the most popular rock group Time Machine was violently criticised by *Komsomolskaya Pravda* (14 April 1982), the organ of the Young Communist League, in a clear attempt to destroy its credibility and popularity among Soviet youth. It was hinted that the group were un-Russian and effeminate.

The harsher line against dissent, opposition and corruption were part of an all-round tightening up by the KGB. Direct dialling from the West was restricted, Soviet citizens were warned against unofficial contacts with Westerners, and those from the West who wished to take Soviet books, bought for roubles, out of the country had first to acquire an export licence.

The tougher policy adopted by the KGB continued after Yuri Andropov stepped down as chairman in May 1982. He was succeeded by Colonel General Vitaly Fedorchuk, until then head of the KGB in the Ukraine. Fedorchuk had been particularly severe on religious believers, nationalists and those who expressed liberal ideas, and was markedly successful in suppressing public demonstrations of opposition to communist rule. It is fair to assume that Andropov also saw Ustinov as a natural ally in his race to the top.

One of the reasons for the lack of a clear favourite to succeed Brezhnev was the skilful way in which the Secretary General prevented one emerging. In 1980 Andrei Kirilenko gained prominence and appeared to be the front runner but was quickly overtaken by Konstantin Chernenko. It was unfortunate for Chernenko that Mikhail Suslov died in January 1982. Not only was the Politburo and the Secretariat shorn of a key figure but the person who would have played a decisive role in the selection of Brezhnev's successor was removed from the scene. Rumoured to have turned down the post of party leader in 1964, Suslov was not motivated by a desire for personal power but was content to act as the ideological conscience of the revolution. His death left a key position vacant in the Secretariat, that of secretary for ideological matters. The man who stepped into his shoes turned out to be Yuri Andropov but he did not return to the Secretariat until May

1982. At the same time Vladimir Dolgikh, the CC secretary for heavy industry, became a candidate member of the Politburo.

Also in May 1982 Chernenko's *Selected Speeches and Writings* were published in English by Pergamon Press, an honour which had not been accorded Kirilenko. Since Chernenko's musings were unlikely to be a commercial success in the West, the decision to provide a hard currency subsidy to secure their publication in English must have been taken at the top in Moscow. Then in stepped Andropov, confirming the trend of Brezhnev's last years – no sooner does a favourite appear than another man pops up with even better credentials.

The ideal candidate for the post of Secretary General would be: about 60 years of age; in good health; Russian; and a full member of the Politburo. He should also have had a higher technical education; spent most of his career in party work although some government work would be an advantage; been First Secretary in an important oblast or republic; spent several years in the CC Secretariat; had experience of industry, agriculture, nationality affairs and foreign affairs; established contacts with the KGB and the military. And he should now occupy a key post in the CC Secretariat or be Prime Minister or President; be acceptable to the majority of Politburo members; be judged neither a convinced conservative nor reformer but appear to be a centrist; be an effective administrator with some leadership qualities; have built up a good 'tail' or 'family circle' of supporters among bureaucratic and functional élites; and be based in Moscow or Leningrad or other important heavy industry region of the RSFSR (Hodnett 1975: 16).

Of course no one existed who united all these qualities in his person, since if there had been one, Brezhnev would have removed him from the Politburo.

According to these criteria Andropov was better qualified than Chernenko. Born in 1914 in the North Caucasus, he attended a technical college and graduated in water transport engineering before working in a small shipbuilding concern in Rybinsk on the Volga. He then became an organiser for the Komsomol (the Young Communist League) in Yaroslavl oblast, where he had received his further education. Next be became the head of the Komsomol in the Karelo–Finnish Republic in 1940. He was involved in the 'guerrilla movement' during the Winter War with Finland and during the Great Patriotic War. He then became second secretary of the CPSU in Petrozavodsk, near Leningrad, in 1944 and in 1947 was appointed second party secretary in Karelia. He was then transferred to work in the CC Secretariat in Moscow in 1951, clear evidence of his success in consolidating Soviet power in Karelia. In 1953 he moved out of the Secretariat to become Soviet *chargé d'affaires* and a year later ambassador to Hungary. In his case this was not a demotion. All Soviet ambassadors to socialist countries come from the CPSU apparatus.

He proved himself a ruthless executor of Soviet interests during the events of 1956. He offered safe conduct to the Prime Minister Imre Nagy and the Defence Minister Pal Maléter but both were arrested and later shot. Moscow was pleased with his performance in Budapest and in 1957 he returned to the Soviet capital to become head of a CC department in the Secretariat responsible for relations with ruling communist parties. In 1962 he was elected a member of the CC, having become a CC secretary the year before. Then in 1967 he was made chairman of the KGB and, in keeping with the status of this office, was elected a candidate member of the Politburo. In 1973 he was made a full member of the Politburo. He remained as the Soviet Union's number one political policeman until May 1982, when he returned to the Secretariat, a move which was vital to his claims for the leadership after Brezhnev's death, since the Secretary General is head of the Secretariat as well as being chairman of the Politburo. Hence he has technical training and Komsomol, party, government (KGB), diplomatic, and international experience.

When Leonid Ilich Brezhnev died on 10 November 1982, the news was withheld until the following day. Andropov and his supporters used this time to seize the succession and this became clear when Andropov was named chairman of the funeral commission on 11 November. The following day an extraordinary CC plenum elected Yuri Andropov Secretary General. The man who proposed his nomination was, appropriately, his defeated rival, Konstantin Chernenko who took the opportunity to remind the new leader of the importance of collective leadership.

The rise of Andropov focuses attention on the role of the political police in the Soviet political system. During the last three succession struggles, the current or former head of the KGB has tried to seize the succession for himself. After Stalin's death it was Lavrenty Beria; after Khrushchev's removal it was Aleksandr Shelepin; and after Brezhnev's death it was Yuri Andropov. Beria was considered so dangerous by his colleagues that he was shot; Shelepin and the then head of the KGB, Vladimir Semichastny, played key roles in the coup against Khrushchev but Shelepin was considered too ambitious for comfort and was gradually eased out of the leadership: Andropov was the first to acquire the post of party leader.

Andropov is the best educated party leader since Lenin, speaking four languages, including English. Again one has to go back to Lenin to find someone who could do this. All party leaders since Lenin have had military experience, albeit as political commissars, but here Andropov is again like the first Bolshevik leader, having spent the war in party work and participated in the 'guerrilla movement'. As head of the

KGB, he headed a paramilitary organisation. However, at 68 he is a good ten years older than Brezhnev was when he took over as party leader, and so is unlikely to survive the 1980s.

Andropov in power

When Andropov took over, he did not enjoy the discretionary power of an American President or a British Prime Minister to alter the personnel of top policy-making bodies. No one was obliged to resign just because there was a new party leader. This is because there is no constitutional definition of the power of the Secretary General or even of the Prime Minister or President. Also no device was agreed during Brezhnev's last years which would have made it possible to transfer power from Brezhnev to his successor. Hence at the end of Brezhnev's rule there was factionalism in the Politburo. When Andropov took over, it was only as head of a faction, albeit one enjoying a majority in the Politburo. Since the office of party leader does not automatically afford him the right to make changes and to replace the Brezhnevites with his own nominees, he has to deploy his political skills to increase his authority in the Politburo. Most of his energies have to be devoted to securing his institutional base in the party apparatus – and thereby building up a position from which to launch policy initiatives. The goal towards which every Secretary General strives is to become more important than all the other members of the Politburo put together, but it is obviously not in the interests of the other members to allow this to happen.

Changes will therefore be gradual as the new leader builds up his power base. The first demotion was predictable: Andrei Kirilenko was dropped from the Politburo at a CC plenum on 22 November 1982. Only one new man was promoted to full membership of the Politburo, Geidar Aliev, First Secretary of the CP of Azerbaidzhan. The first Azerbaidzhani to become a full member of the Politburo, he increases the proportion of non-Slavs in the supreme party body to a quarter – the others being the Kazakh, Kunaev, and the Latvian, Pelshe. More significantly he was a career KGB officer and was head of the political police in Azerbaidzhan from 1967 until he became party leader in 1969. Then the USSR Supreme Soviet meeting on 23–25 November 1982 elected him first deputy Prime Minister of the USSR. The incumbent Prime Minister, Nikolai Tikhonov, is 77 and the first deputy Ivan Arkhipov is 75. Aliev at 59 is clearly being groomed for the position of USSR Prime Minister. The same meeting also made Andropov a member of the presidium of the USSR Supreme Soviet, a position he would need to occupy to be elected President. This step, however, was not taken, and the deputy President, Vasili Kuznetsov, continues to act as President.

Andropov's main power base is the CC Secretariat, and here he will wish to remove those whom he regards as too closely identified with his predecessor and place his own men in key positions. The main post is that concerned with cadres, since control of appointments is of major significance. Chernenko is at present head of the General Department but Andropov will wish to replace his defeated rival as soon as possible with his own nominee. Since patronage and privilege are endemic in Soviet life, a politician seeks to promote those with whom he has successfully worked previously. In this way promotion came to many who were connected with Brezhnev. Over the years 1953–74, 24 cadres from Dnepropetrovsk oblast in the Ukraine, where Brezhnev had worked, gained faster promotion than any similar group from any other oblast, for instance. Members of the family also move upwards. Yuri Brezhnev, the former Secretary General's son, for example, is first Deputy Minister of Foreign Trade. As the Secretary General seeks to fill the Politburo with his own nominees, he must ensure that the various bureaucracies and functional élites are in balance since this makes his position more secure. A sure sign of his upward mobility is when a cult of his personality begins to flower.

Policy options

During his years in the KGB Andropov sought to take the pulse of Soviet society. He needed an accurate picture of what people in all walks of life were thinking and what motivated them. The political police kept a particularly close eye on the creative and technical intelligentsia, had a say in what was published and exhibited, and saw the rise of the secondary or black economy with mixed feelings. The new Secretary General is fully aware that the Soviet Union is at a crossroads. Marxism–Leninism, the ruling ideology, is no longer the mobilising and inspirational force it once was. Brezhnev conceded that its presentation was dull and lifeless. How is it to be revitalised?

The present slowdown in economic growth has made many bureaucrats pessimistic about satisfying the rising expectations of the population. Socialism promises unlimited progress, ever-increasing living standards and the elimination of all dull, boring and repetitive work.

Yuri Davidov became a very popular Russian philosopher in the late 1970s. He viewed the concept of economic success as alien to Russian culture. He blamed the 19th century Russian socialists for introducing the idea of an ever-increasing standard of living and culture. The communists then continued this myth making. In his opinion, socialism has lost its moral values due to consumerism. Dull, repetitive work should be seen as truly ethical, moral labour. To Davidov it is a short step from killing one's neighbour to ensure personal economic success – described in the pages of Dostoevsky – to killing one's neighbour for the economic success of society. If one suppresses the moral, ethical being within oneself, one is killing oneself. The rush for growth has led to a blind eye being turned to that law breaking which results in plan fulfilment. This is anathema to those who see such behaviour as leading to the destruction of traditional Russian values. Reverting to the ideology, communism cannot be built unless new men and women come into being in socialist society who will personify moral and ethical values.

The army of bureaucrats, political policemen and military officers are searching for an ideology to justify and give meaning to their present role and to ensure that it continues. Marxism–Leninism places power in the hands of the working class, something which does not serve the interests of these élites. One solution is to rehabilitate the state. Marxism abhors the state and envisages its eventual demise. Its rehabilitation began under Lenin and Stalin but Khrushchev reversed this process. This is one of the reasons why he is so greatly disliked by the Soviet establishment. Khrushchev believed that the socialist system was superior to capitalism and that people would work for moral reasons. Hence he was too inclined to believe that workers would automatically be willing to work. He diminished the power of the state by decentralising economic decision-making and promoting autonomous social institutions. His leap into communism in 1961 made the bureaucrats profoundly ill at ease since it pointed to their eventual redundancy. The establishment found him guilty of 'ethical voluntarism'. Brezhnev reversed this trend, and under him the power of the state mounted and the all people's state was promoted.

Kosygin was never popular, since he was linked to 'economic pragmatism', something which the bureaucrats found painful. It raised expectations and tried to increase efficiency. Poland rushed for growth in the 1970s with disastrous consequences. In the Soviet Union it led to the flowering of the secondary economy and the appearance of the *nouveaux riches*. It appears that CC members and their families have to give the specialist a 'present' if they are to receive the medical treatment they desire in the special CC clinic. Previously this was one of the privileges of office they were able to enjoy, without paying of course. These bureaucrats would like to see a clampdown on corruption and the suppression of the *nouveaux riches*. The intelligentsia are not keen to see an expansion of their numbers and would prefer access to higher education to be further restricted. Ideally they would like the size of the intelligentsia to remain constant thus ensuring that they diminish as a proportion of Soviet society due to the growth of population, in order to retain their élite status.

Who is to blame for the slowdown in economic growth? One cannot be seen to blame the leadership or the communist party or the state.

That leaves the working class. It is depressing to have to blame the labour force for the ills of the country but there is no other scapegoat. Books and plays purvey the view that anyone involved in the consumer syndrome cannot be improved morally or ethically. A play called *Bonus*, and seen by Brezhnev, concerned a worker who rejected his bonus for plan fulfilment because it had been achieved dishonestly.

A view which is gaining currency is that society is corrupt but the state is ethical. Virtue resides in the state, and a new state ideology is needed to replace working class ideology. Andropov is well aware of what the ruling class in the Soviet Union is thinking and he is even rumoured to have a private collection of icons and to enjoy modern jazz. He neatly illustrates the schizophrenia which is now in evidence among the Soviet élite.

There is plenty of scope for innovation in industry and agriculture. Some changes in economic administration were to have been ready for the 26th Party Congress in February–March 1981 but never appeared. Clearly they contained emendations which powerful interests perceived as being dangerous to their position. A decentralisation of economic decision making in an enterprise reduces the influence of the planners, administrators and local party officials. It is also a moot point whether many plant managers would relish additional powers. A fundamental reform would oblige them to cease being administrators and become managers. Since the central party and government bureaucrats dominate decision making, they are perfectly placed to defend their own interests. However an aspiring leader must be keenly concerned with economic success and raising living standards, since this creates optimism and adds credibility to his ideology. If the economy continues to falter and social tensions increase, the Secretary General's position will become difficult, if not precarious. The experience of Eastern Europe, especially Poland, reveals that the leader prefers to concentrate on staying in power rather than risk removal over fundamental economic reforms.

The promotion of Geidar Aliev would indicate that no fundamental economic reforms are on the horizon. As Prime Minister he would lack the economic and engineering expertise to make independent judgments. His skills are administrative and organisational. It would not be surprising if other high-ranking KGB officials, who had proved themselves under Andropov, were promoted to high state positions. On the other hand, promotions to the Secretariat are likely to come from within the party apparatus itself.

What are the options available to Andropov in agriculture? Emphasis on the private plot could be continued and expanded. However, so far, it has not led to any marked increase in the amount of marketed food. Then garages and services such as restaurants and laundries could be handed over to the private sector. This would certainly increase consumer satisfaction. The main drawback to moves in this direction is that they would vastly expand the private and secondary economies. It would also fuel corruption. Workers would resent seeing peasants enjoying higher living standards than themselves, and if incomes were higher in the private sector, why should a skilled worker stay in the state sector? The party apparatus and the KGB would both oppose such developments since they would reduce the influence of the former and multiply the work load of the latter.

Foreign policy will occupy much of the time of the new Secretary General. After previous leadership changes, the new team has always adopted a conciliatory attitude towards the outside world. The Austrian State treaty of 1955 was a tangible fruit of peaceful coexistence after Stalin, and détente gradually emerged under Brezhnev. Andropov has begun by making conciliatory gestures towards the Chinese and has indicated that improved Soviet–American relations would be welcome. However the Chinese want deeds, not words. They want, among other things, a reduction of Soviet troops on their border and the withdrawal of Soviet troops from Afghanistan. Then there is the impasse in Poland, but Andropov will make it clear to the Poles that, after martial law has been lifted, there can be no going back to Solidarność. Communist power will be seen to be immovable, even though the economic price of keeping such an unrepresentative minority in power is high.

The indications are that Andropov will pursue a policy which favours the interests of the bureaucrats with few fundamental changes. More emphasis can be placed on the state and a campaign against corruption, drunkenness, absenteeism and social misdemeanours could be waged. This would please the bureaucrats and confer greater authority on the KGB. Hence the influence of the security police is likely to rise, as is that of the military.

This scenario could turn out to be incorrect for two reasons: a crisis in foreign policy and/or economic failure. It is even conceivable that both could occur at the same time. War in the Middle East, or conflict with the United States, would require a party leader to be capable of working 18 or more hours a day for an extended period *and* hold his own in discussions about policy. If the leadership perceived that economic decline could raise social tensions above an acceptable level, then radical economic policies might be adopted. The first priority of all policy is, after all, to sustain the political élite in power, even if this involves unorthodox measures. Ideology, when all is said and done, serves the party, not the other way round. A danger for the Soviet Union is that in the past aspiring leaders have not shied away from damaging the country internally and externally, in the short term, in their bid for leadership. Khrushchev did, for example, when he dethroned Stalin in 1956. The record, however, shows that in the long term the leader acts in the national interest, whereas an aspiring leader tends to act in his own personal interest.

Stalin and Khrushchev were innovative in economic policy and took enormous risks. Brezhnev, when he became leader in the late 1960s, only needed to continue along the well-trodden path of favouring heavy at the expense of light industry. He also continued the trend, started by Khrushchev, of increasing capital investment in agriculture. His successors will have to solve the problem of how to switch from extensive to intensive growth, since the plentiful supplies of raw materials and labour are no longer available. Brezhnev did not really tackle the problem of raising labour productivity. Now it is Andropov's turn to try.

Since Andropov, it would appear, has entered into a tactical alliance with the armed forces could he become the prisoner of the military?

The communist party has always been on its guard against Bonapartist tendencies among the military. It started with Trotsky, and the bloody purges of 1937–8 were designed to eliminate any opposition to Stalin's policies. In the post-war period the most intriguing figure is Marshal Georgy Zhukov. He played a key role in transporting Khrushchev's supporters to the Kremlin in June 1957, but the First Secretary soon came to the conclusion that he was dispensable. Marshal F. Golikov, at the 22nd Party Congress in 1962, was very frank about what was happening in the army under Zhukov's leadership:

> Party criticism about shortcomings in the conduct and the work of communist commanders at all levels was forbidden in the army . . . Attempts were made to evade . . . control by the Central Committee, to undermine the influence of the party and to cut the army and the navy off from the party and the people. A cult of Zhukov's person was initiated. There was a growing drift to unlimited authority in the army and the country.
>
> (Protocol of 22nd Party Congress)

One should take much of this with a grain of salt since it represents *ex post facto* vilification of Zhukov but the point being clearly made to the military was that the party would not countenance any independence on the part of the armed forces.

Andropov is well aware that the military will expect ever rising defence expenditure, but more investment may be needed in the civilian sectors of the economy to head off social conflict. Andropov can then either use the instruments of coercion to suppress any unrest, or switch resources and accept conflict with the military. He is more likely to choose the former option.

Since Andropov is unlikely to survive the 1980s as leader, the struggle for succession will begin again in the near future. A younger generation of leaders, formed in the post-Stalin era, will gradually emerge and one of them may be the next party leader. Be that as it may, Andropov's leadership will see an increase in the influence of the KGB and the military and these two institutions will have a major, if not dominant, say in who succeeds Andropov. The younger generation may find that their options for fundamental innovation have been sharply circumscribed by the time they have climbed to the top.

Addendum
Andropov is a Russian surname and is probably formed from the surname Antropov under the influence of Russian names beginning in Andr–. Antropov itself is derived from the baptismal (first or Christian) name Antrop with the addition of the suffix –ov. Antrop, in turn, is a colloquial form, along with Antropiy and Evtrop of the baptismal name Evtropiy which is the name in Russian corresponding to the Greek first name Eutropios. The latter is formed from the Greek adjective eutropos, which in Ancient Greek means either 'versatile' or 'of good disposition'. Hence the name came into Russian after the introduction of Christianity in the 10th century. Andropov was originally a patronymic or the name of the father but when surnames entered Russian it became one. It is likely that Andropov, as a surname, has been in use for 300–400 years. Hence Yuri Vladimirovich Andropov is Russian with an adopted Greek name and can either be called Mr Versatile or Yuri of the Good Disposition.

The present Soviet leadership (November 1982):

Members of the Politburo	*Current responsibility*
Andropov, Yu. V. (1914)	Secretary General, chairman of the Defence Council
Aliev, G.A. (1923)	First deputy Prime Minister
Chernenko, K.U. (1911)	CC secretary, head of General Department
Gorbachev, M.S. (1931)	CC secretary, for agriculture
Grishin, V.V. (1914)	First Secretary, Moscow city party organisation
Gromyko, A.A. (1909)	USSR Minister of Foreign Affairs
Kunaev, D.A. (1912)	First Secretary, CP of Kazakhstan
Pelshe, A. Ye. (1899)	Chairman, Party Control Commission
Romanov, G.V. (1923)	First Secretary, Leningrad oblast party organisation
Shcherbitsky, V.V. (1918)	First Secretary, CP of Ukraine
Tikhonov, N.A. (1905)	Prime Minister

Ustinov, D.F. (1908)   USSR Minister of Defence

Candidate Members of the Politburo

Demichev, P.N. (1918)	USSR Minister of Culture
Dolgikh, V.I. (1924)	CC secretary, heavy industry
Kiselev, T. Ya. (1917)	First Secretary, CP of Belorussia
Kuznetsov, V.V. (1901)	Deputy (acting) President
Ponomarev, B.N. (1905)	CC secretary, head, International Department
Rashidov, Sh. R. (1917)	First Secretary, CP of Uzbekistan
Shevardnadze, E.A. (1928)	First Secretary, CP of Georgia
Solomentsev, M.S. (1913)	Prime Minister, RSFSR

Secretariat

Andropov, Yu. V.	as above
Chernenko, K.U.	"
Gorbachev, M.S.	"
Dolgikh, V.I.	"
Ponomarev, B.N.	"
Ryzhkov, N.I. (1929)	head, economic functionaries
Kapitonov, I.V. (1915)	head, organisational party work
Zimyanin, M.V. (1914)	head, ideology, propaganda, culture
Rusakov, K.V. (1909)	head, liaison with communist and workers' parties of socialist countries

(In official Soviet publications full and candidate members of the Politburo are given in alphabetical order but members of the Secretariat are given in order of rank.)

Presidium, USSR Council of Ministers

Tikhonov, N.A.	Prime Minister
Aliev, G.A.	First deputy Prime Minister
Arkhipov, I.V.	First deputy Prime Minister
Antonov, A.K.	uncertain
* Baibakov, N.K.	Chairman, State Planning Commission
Bodyul, I.I.	uncertain
Dymshits, V.E.	General Questions
Kostandov, L.A.	Comecon Affairs
Makeev, V.N.	uncertain
* Marchuk, G.I.	Chairman, State Committee for Science and Technology

* Martynov, N.V.	Chairman, State Committee for Material and Technical Supply
* Novikov, I.T.	Chairman, State Committee for Construction
Nuriev, Z.N.	uncertain
Smirnov, L.V.	Chairman, Military–Industrial Committee
Talyzin, N.V.	USSR representative to Comecon

* Deputy Prime Minister

3 Dissent, Opposition and Instability
Iain Elliot

How serious a threat does internal opposition pose to the stability of the Soviet regime? Assessing the numbers and the significance of those who oppose the prevailing system might well seem impossible. Especially when the main source of information about the Soviet Union – the controlled press – repeatedly asserts in front page editorials that the 'entire Soviet people unanimously supports the foreign and domestic policies of the Communist Party of the Soviet Union (CPSU)', while only occasionally admitting in brief back page reports that political opponents have been executed.

There are, however, additional sources of information: the first-hand reports of visitors to the USSR; the experience of Soviet citizens who have left the Soviet Union; and the 'self-published' documents (*samizdat*) of people in the USSR who cannot find a forum in the official media. By the end of 1981, the reliable *Samizdat Archive* in Munich contained some 5,000 numbered items. Such varied evidence allows one to assert with conviction that dissent and opposition to communist party rule persist and deserve further study.

It is much more difficult to determine whether there are enough dedicated opponents of the regime to cause instability, or indeed if there are other factors which might combine to threaten the future of the one-party Soviet state. Biographical details of more than 10,000 dissidents in the Soviet Union are known (see, for example, de Boer *et al.* 1982), but the total population of the Soviet Union exceeds 270 million. A distinction can be drawn between opposition – a drive by those hostile to the system to replace the existing rulers, and dissent – an attempt merely to reform the system by those who object to certain policies and doctrines.

However, when the regime functions on the principle that 'he who is not with us is against us' such distinctions tend to become blurred. Some dissidents, who in the 1970s openly joined in the struggle for human rights based on the Soviet constitution and various international agreements, had by the 1980s become disillusioned after waves of arrests decimated the movement, and several expressed the belief that clandestine opposition movements might prove more effective. In September 1982 the Helsinki monitoring group gave up the unequal struggle and disbanded, further illustration of this point of view.

Does a fertile soil exist in which dissent and opposition might spread from the few thousand activists to the millions of ordinary citizens about whom so little is known? A glance at Soviet history gives some insight into the probable attitude of the masses. The only even partially democratic elections to be held since Lenin seized power (the elections to the Constituent Assembly in November 1917) gave the Bolsheviks less than a quarter of the votes, and in the Civil War which followed, Lenin and his followers were violently opposed by virtually every other political grouping, whether conservative, liberal, socialist, anarchist, or any of the many other varieties. This opposition did not disappear with the last battle of the Civil War, nor did the non-Russian nations lose their aspirations to independence when Lenin ordered the Red Army to crush the nationalist governments in the Ukraine, Trans-caucasia and Central Asia.

The Baltic states won their independence in 1920, but just two decades later were forcibly incorporated into the USSR. Nationalist guerrillas were still fighting Soviet Army units in Estonia, Latvia, Lithuania and the Ukraine in the 1950s. Soviet publicists now argue that 'the Soviet people' are against war because 20 million Soviet citizens were killed in the struggle against Nazi Germany. Although this figure is probably an exaggeration, since immediately after the war a figure of 7.5 million was officially quoted, the basic argument is sound. It can equally be argued that the people of the USSR are against the political system that resulted in the Stalinist purges which were responsible for the death of 20 million – and in this case the figure is possibly an underestimation.

Hundreds of thousands of Russian prisoners of war agreed to join the 'Army of Liberation' formed by the Germans to fight against Stalin under the command of General Andrei Vlasov, a decorated Soviet general who before his capture had commanded the Second Army defending Moscow. Similar formations were recruited from among Ukrainian, Caucasian, Tartar and Central Asian prisoners. Few of the large numbers of former Soviet citizens displaced to Western Europe during the war wished to return to the USSR.

Indeed, even today, whenever a section of the Soviet population is given the opportunity of leaving its homeland, people go in great numbers. Hundreds of thousands of Jews, ethnic Germans and Armenians have emigrated in recent years, and, to judge by the number of aircraft hijackings, or 'defections' by Soviet citizens permitted to travel abroad, those who have been allowed to emigrate are but a small percentage of the discontented masses who wish to opt out of Soviet society.

The tight restrictions on travel abroad and the firmly sealed borders appear to confirm this conclusion. Despite the severe penalties imposed on those detected attempting to leave the USSR unofficially, the large number of 'defectors' includes representatives of a wide range of social and professional groups, from ordinary sailors who have jumped ship to privileged world-famous artists who have come to the West on tours aimed at raising the prestige of the USSR: there are even defectors among the Soviet élite: Stalin's daughter Svetlana is among the best known of these. Few other states in the history of humanity have gone to such lengths to keep their citizens at home, yet the exodus continues.

If, as is argued, discontent with Soviet society is widespread, how does it find expression, and how great a threat to stability is it likely to be? There is little possibility that any indication of dissatisfaction will emerge in the official electoral process. Only one candidate, carefully selected by the party, is permitted to stand in each constituency and it is claimed that these officially approved candidates receive 99.99 per cent of the votes cast by the loyal electorate. After the 1979 elections to the USSR Supreme Soviet, it was claimed that

results of the elections to the country's highest organ of state bear witness to the convincing victory of the indestructible bloc of communist and non-party candidates. By their unanimous voting for the candidates, the Soviet people have expressed their fervent approval and undivided support for the domestic and foreign policies of the Communist Party and the Soviet state.

(*Pravda* 6 March 1979)

Attempts by the 'Election 79' group to nominate dissidents Roy Medvedev and Lyudmila Agapova to stand against official candidates were quickly nullified by the authorities.

Real power resides not in the USSR Supreme Soviet, but in the top party bodies, the Central Committee, Secretariat and Politburo, which are not in theory subordinated to the votes of the electorate.

No constitutional procedure for renewing membership of the top party organs, or for choosing a successor to Leonid Brezhnev as Secretary General of the party, was established at the 26th Party Congress in February–March 1981. As the aged leaders die off, the possibility of factional conflict in the Politburo seems certain to increase. While this in itself may not be a major threat to stability, it can weaken the leadership's ability to deal effectively with other challenges.

The way the leaders are projected does little to bridge the gulf between them and the population. In the 1970s Brezhnev was portrayed in the media as a war hero; his memoirs were widely publicised and even partially set to music. In general, the secrecy surrounding the leaders' private life fosters widespread belief in even the most outrageous allegations about their personal habits.

An example will illustrate this. In early 1982 a scandal broke out in Moscow when a singer in the Bolshoi Theatre was arrested during an investigation into the theft of diamonds from a Moscow circus performer. The singer was rumoured to be a 'close friend' of Brezhnev's daughter Galina, married to Lt. General Yury Churbanov, of the Ministry of Internal Affairs. Normally such a relationship would provide immunity from arrest. The story which circulated in Moscow claimed that Semen Tsvigun, First Deputy Chairman of the KGB, himself took the decision to arrest the singer but was subjected to severe criticism by Mikhail Suslov who wished to suppress the scandal. Tsvigun is said to have committed suicide. His obituary (*Izvestiya*, 22 January 1982) was not signed by either Brezhnev or Suslov, whose signatures would normally have been expected in the case of such a prominent member of the Central Committee of the CPSU. Within days of raging at Tsvigun, Suslov suffered a stroke and died.

True or false, such rumours are fostered by the lack of information in the media about the family life of the leaders and illustrate the alienation of the population from the leadership and its ideology. Brezhnev's speech at the 26th Congress of the CPSU in February–March 1981 contained a proposal to draft a new Programme of the CPSU to replace the 1961 version, which promised that by 1980 'the material and technical basis of communism' would have been created in the Soviet Union and that in the production of food and consumer goods the USSR would have overtaken the USA. The new Programme was to lay down general principles rather than give specific predictions; communism was a long-term goal rather than a target which could be attained by 1990.

The ideology is still useful in helping to impose conformity; whatever people may believe, they know what they are supposed to say for the sake of their careers and the well-being of their families. Debate in officially sanctioned publications is limited by the need to couch all arguments in Marxist–Leninist terms. An editorial in *Pravda* (11 May 1979) stated that it was the duty of the media 'brightly to show the greatness of the Communist ideals, the all-conquering strength of Marxism-Leninism', but a Central Committee decree on improving ideological and political education admitted that 'we still have a considerable number of weak points and failings, several of which are very substantial' (*Pravda* 6 May 1979). It continued:

One big failing which substantially reduces the effectiveness of the influence achieved by educational work on the consciousness and emotions of people is the formalism which is frequently encountered – a tendency to babble and verbiage, every kind of propaganda cliché, the grey conventionalism of material, frequent mechanical repetition of generalisations instead of thinking creatively about them and searching for lively and intelligible forms.

Even many committed communists have eventually become totally disillusioned after decades of struggle and suffering. Academician Arnosht Kolman, a colleague of Lenin and member of the CPSU for 58 years, asked for political asylum in Sweden and on 22 September 1976 wrote to Brezhnev, returning his party card: 'I have come to the firm conviction that to stay in the ranks of the CPSU would mean the betrayal of the ideals of social justice, humanitarianism and of building a new, more perfect human society for which I have striven, despite all my mistakes and delusions, throughout my life.'

Of course an unpopular regime and dissatisfied population does not necessarily mean that the stability of the USSR is seriously under threat. What are the challenges to CPSU rule, and how are they controlled?

The military
The only body strong enough to seize power from the party is the military, but the leaders of the armed forces could not be more privileged than they are now, even under a military dictatorship. Defence is allocated a very large slice of the budget, and the military make up about 8 per cent of the total membership of the Central Committee. Some top officers may feel that the military have had less say in formulating Politburo policy since the death of Marshal Grechko, and some may resent the awarding of the highest military rank, Marshal of the Soviet Union, to party leader Brezhnev and Defence Minister Ustinov, but for the most part, the interests of party and military leaders are identical. Khrushchev may have lost the support of the generals over the Cuban crisis and his armament strategy, but Brezhnev allowed heavy investment in both conventional and strategic weapons. He avoided losing face in foreign adventures and Afghanistan is probably regarded as a useful testing ground by the Soviet generals.

Conscripts and lower-ranking officers are more subject to the general dissatisfactions of the Soviet population, and according to eyewitness accounts, morale among the men serving in Afghanistan is low, with drug addiction becoming a problem. Media accounts in the USSR pretended that Soviet forces were seldom directly involved in the fighting, and although by Western accounts they suffered thousands of casualties, these were only rarely reported in the USSR. An exception was made by Mukhamednazar Gapurov, First Secretary of the CP of Turkmenistan which borders on Afghanistan. Wishing to inspire the young people of his republic, he spoke at a Komsomol Congress about communist ideals and continued:

An eternal symbol of fidelity to these ideals and an example of unfading heroism is provided by the bullet-ridden and blood-stained Komsomol card of the 18-year-old lad Khodzhanepes Charyev, a native of Khodzhambas oblast, who perished in battle on 16 September last year, carrying out the sacred duty of a soldier and internationalist. A son of the Turkmen people, a member of the

Komsomol, he was helping to defend the freedom, independence and social progress of fraternal Afghanistan.

(*Turkmenskaya Iskra* 27 March 1982)

The returning conscripts told a different story, but the silence of the controlled media meant that their horror stories and the losses of some Soviet families were unlikely to engender an effective anti-war movement. After the invasion of Czechoslovakia in 1968, there were unsubstantiated reports of small-scale mutinies among returning troops, but party and KGB control tends to be too efficient for such actions to be more than heroic gestures. Life even in peacetime is extremely hard for the ordinary serviceman and there are many cases of desertion, some deserters escaping to the West. Private Igor Alekseichuk crossed the mined border into West Germany; KGB Captain Aleksei Myagkov defected in West Berlin while 'guarding' a busload of Soviet soldiers; in 1976, Senior Lieutenant Belenkov flew his MiG-25 to Japan; in November 1975, the crew of a patrol vessel mutinied and attempted to sail to Sweden, but were prevented by Soviet military aircraft.

Even more significant was the case of Colonel Oleg Penkovsky who offered to spy for the West because he was opposed to CPSU rule; he was discovered and condemned to death in 1963. In January 1969, shots were fired at a column of vehicles carrying astronauts and Soviet leaders; a young lieutenant, Anatoly Ilin, was arrested and declared insane. Later in 1969, several arrests were made by the KGB in connection with an opposition movement involving officers of the Baltic fleet. Three officers were sentenced for organising a Union of Struggle for Political Rights.

Major-General Petr Grigorenko became famous in the 1960s for his criticisms of the regime's undemocratic rule. He warned of the danger of returning to Stalinist methods and was cruelly persecuted for his defence of human rights. Forced into exile, he was deprived of his Soviet citizenship in 1978. Such examples might suggest that the regime cannot fully rely on the loyalty of the armed forces, but individual protests do not necessarily mean that an organised military opposition could arise to threaten CPSU control.

Nationalist pressures

It is part of Soviet philosophy that the 'collapse of colonial empires is determined by the whole course of history' (*Pravda* 24 October 1978), yet to some observers the USSR itself resembles an empire where Russian leaders exercise supreme political dominion over an aggregate of many states. Of course the Soviet Union differs in several important respects from the pre-revolutionary Russian empire. For a start, the non-Russian nations are represented in the supreme organ of power, the Politburo. In summer 1982, for example, the Ukrainian

Shcherbitsky, the Kazakh Kunaev and the Latvian Pelshe were full members, while among the candidate members were Aliev from Azerbaidzhan, Kiselev from Belorussia, Rashidov from Uzbekistan, and Shevardnadze from Georgia. It is argued that under the leadership of the CPSU, the hundred-plus nationalities in the USSR have been united in one happy family: 'By all its actions the Party educates the working people in the spirit of Soviet patriotism and socialist internationalism, in the proud feeling of belonging to one great Soviet Homeland' (*Pravda* 5 July 1982).

Yet while the proportion of Russians in the population of the USSR is falling (according to the census returns, from 54.6 per cent in 1959 to 52.4 per cent in 1979) their share of important posts has been rising. For instance, at the 23rd CPSU Congress in 1966, Russians accounted for 57 per cent of the Central Committee membership; at the 26th Congress in 1981, their share had grown to 68 per cent. In the non-Russian republics the vital 'watch-dog' post of Second Secretary is normally filled by a Russian sent from the central apparatus in Moscow. Russian, hailed as the 'language of Lenin', is a compulsory subject in every school and is frequently promoted at the expense of the native language.

The spread of Russian traditions and culture puts the national heritage of the minorities at risk. In Latvia and Estonia, the influx of Russians is a cause of conflict. Latvians have dropped from 62 per cent of the total population of their republic in 1959 to below 54 per cent in 1979, while Russians have increased from 27 to 33 per cent. The same trend is evident is Estonia, while in Kazakhstan, although this trend is reversed, there are still more Russians (41 per cent) than Kazakhs (36 per cent). Many in the republics resent the way that all major policy decisions are taken in Moscow, even when the main effect will be felt in a particular republic rather than in the USSR as a whole.

In some cases protesters appear to be given discreet encouragement even by individual local Party officials, but the regime's policy remains one of unrelenting hostility to what is regarded as 'bourgeois nationalism'. In his 26th Congress speech Brezhnev said: 'The CPSU has struggled and will always act decisively against such phenomena, alien to the nature of socialism, as chauvinism or nationalism.' The available evidence of nationalist opposition to Moscow rule varies in quantity and quality among the hundred or more non-Russian nations in the USSR, which range in size from the 42 million Ukrainians to distinct national groups of less than a thousand people. In the Ukrainian, Baltic and Transcaucasian republics there are frequent protests against communist policies.

Ukraine

The guerrilla operations of the Ukrainian Insurgent Army (UPA) were crushed by Soviet forces in the early 1950s, but the UPA and its political wing, the Organisation of Ukrainian Nationalists, which is active among the thousands of émigré Ukrainians, are repeatedly subjected to virulent attacks in the official media. Executions of Ukrainians accused of collaborating with the German occupation forces were still taking place some 40 years after the alleged atrocities had been committed.

The Ukrainian National Front (UNF) was crushed by the KGB in 1966, after 15 issues of its journal *The Motherland and Liberty* had appeared. The UNF sent a memorandum to the 23rd CPSU Congress demanding independence for the Ukraine. The last known issues of the *Ukrainian Herald*, the main clandestine publication in the republic, appeared in 1974. Its authors express bitter oppositon to Russian domination, accusing the 'Kremlin colonisers' of robbing the Ukraine of manpower and resources to develop remote areas in the far north and attack the nationalities policy of the 'party bureaucratic apparatus':

A new fable has been created in the Kremlin about a 'new historical community, the Soviet people'. Who needs this abstract cover, under which the Russian chauvinistic backbone hides? It is high time for the Russian imperialists to realise that it is the Russian empire that has become outmoded, although it was touched up with a new coat of red paint in 1917. Because the enslaved peoples of the Russian empire do exist and are fighting for their independence, although in unbelievably harsh and complicated circumstances. And this struggle will grow more intense with time, irrespective of whatever terror the occupiers may use, because the illusions born of October 1917 about the possibility of national and social liberation within the boundaries of a centralised, multi-national Russian state have been completely dispelled. (See the translation of issue 7–8 published by Smoloskyp, Baltimore, 1976, p. 75).

Since the late 1960s the KGB has put great effort into suppressing the most articulate proponents of Ukrainian separatism, and even those who actively promoted Ukrainian culture were subjected to harassment and arrest. The journalist Vyacheslav Chornovil (born 1937) protested at the treatment of Ukrainian intellectuals whose trials he covered in 1965. His exposé (published in English as *The Chornovil Papers*, New York, 1968) and his other protest writings and dissident activities brought him over 15 years imprisonment. He was re-sentenced in 1980 on a fabricated charge. The historian Valentyn Moroz (born 1939) had already served four years in labour camps when he was re-sentenced in 1970, but after worldwide protests at his brutal treatment in prison was released to the United States in 1979 along with three other well-known dissidents in exchange for captured Soviet spies. Chornovil, Moroz and many others have provided rich documentation on the strong pride of the Ukrainians in their nationhood, with which the policies of the Soviet leadership come into conflict.

With the ousting of Petr Shelest, criticised as being too sympathetic to Ukrainian nationalism, and his replacement as First Secretary of the CP of the Ukraine by Vladimir Shcherbitsky in 1972, the repression was intensified. Political arrests continued into the 1980s; according to a *samizdat* report, Vitaly Fedorchuk, then head of the Ukrainian KGB, boasted in April 1981 that in the previous year '40 Ukrainian nationalists were rendered harmless. To avoid unnecessary international fuss most of them were sentenced as common criminals.' Dissident sources reported mass disturbances early in 1981 in Ivano-Frankivsk in Western Ukraine, where crowds demanded better food supplies and independence for the Ukraine.

Baltic States

Although all three – Estonia, Latvia and Lithuania – lost their independence when they were incorporated in the USSR in 1940, evidence of separatism is much stronger in Lithuania and Estonia than in Latvia. In August 1979 a group of 45 Lithuanians, Latvians and Estonians issued an appeal to the United Nations to recognise the right of their countries to self-determination and independence.

In *Lithuania* clandestine publications are more widespread than in any other non-Russian republic; the combination of nationalism and religious faith makes dissent more of a mass movement than in the Ukraine, and as it resembles opposition trends in neighbouring Poland, it is a particular cause of concern to the Soviet leadership. In 1982 the *Chronicle of the Lithuanian Catholic Church* marked its tenth anniversary; despite every effort by the KGB to suppress it, over 50 issues had appeared documenting in detail the persecution of religious believers and the suppression of the country's national heritage.

Even more nationalist in content is *Auśra* (The Dawn); issue 28 (dated September 1981) recalled the death of Romas Kalanta, whose self-immolation in May 1972 started large-scale riots in Kaunas:

This young man, who flamed like a torch in the Soviet night, represented a cry for help to the world: save Lithuania, help it to free itself! The occupying power and its collaborators were seized with fear – a nineteen-year-old youth was not afraid of the apparatus of enslavement; he unleashed a public protest by burning himself to death.

Issue 30 of *Auśra* (March 1982) denounced the occupation of Afghanistan:

For almost three years blood has been spilled in Afghanistan. After invading a quiet land, unaffected by any political struggle, the occupiers launched a fratricidal war. Representatives of other nations are also forced to participate in this war: Ukrainians, Estonians, Latvians, Lithuanians. Under oppression themselves, they must obey the brutal orders of the Russian officers, and shed both their own and Afghan blood.

According to the clandestine publication *Varpas* (The Bell), there is a Revolutionary Front of Lithuania which aims at the withdrawal of Soviet troops from Lithuania and the holding of free elections under United Nations supervision. *Tautos Kelias* (The Path of the Nation) is a strongly nationalist but scholarly *samizdat* journal which first appeared in 1980; it deals with economic and demographic problems as well as making overtly nationalist statements: 'The victims of jails and concentration camps and the blood of those who perished fighting as partisans oblige us to accomplish that for which they died – the reestablishment of a free and independent Lithuania.'

In *Estonia* the Party First Secretary Karl Vaino complained of 'particularly glaring manifestations of blinkered national attitudes on the part of ideologically and politically immature people' (*Sovetskaya Estoniya* 29 January 1981). There have been many cases in recent years of young people receiving short prison sentences for raising the national flag of independent Estonia and on several occasions civil disturbances have manifested nationalist feelings. In September–October 1980 demonstrations developed after a mass protest at a football match on 22 September when a pop group was prevented from singing nationalist songs at half-time. Other disturbances followed in Tallinn, Pärnu and Tartu, mainly involving students and school children protesting about school conditions, but shouting of nationalist slogans was also reported.

On 13 October Radio Tallinn announced that 'in connection with the gross violation of public order recently committed in Tallinn the Estonian SSR Public Prosecutor's Office has instituted criminal proceedings against the instigators of these disturbances and against malicious hooligans'. A group of 40 prominent writers, poets, scientists and actors wrote an open letter in which they expressed concern that growing fears about national identity would lead to further conflict between Russians and Estonians.

Appeals to the West for support in gaining independence were issued by the Estonian Democratic Movement but were answered by increased arrests and trials. Sergei Soldatov, imprisoned in 1975 for his part in the democratic movement, was released in January 1981 and exiled to the West in May. Another leading dissident, Juri Kukk (born 1948) who was imprisoned in January 1981 for allegedly disseminating 'knowingly false fabrications discrediting the Soviet political and social system' died in March after brutal force-feeding to break his hunger strike.

In *Latvia* too there have been separatist groups, although *samizdat* materials are less in evidence. In April 1962 an underground nationalist organisation of young Latvians called the Baltic Federation was broken by the KGB, and in June 1976 an open letter signed by the Lativan Democratic Youth Committee and the Latvian Independence Movement protested at Russification and supported the struggle for self-determination of all Soviet-dominated nations. In 1972 an open letter from 17 disillusioned Latvian communists emerged, condemning the decline in the use of Latvian among party cadres and administrators in the republic. The government was accused of concealing economic and social shortcomings with 'deliberate distortions and outright lies'. The letter continued: 'Those who dare to object not only lose their positions but also their freedom, and often end up suffering sub-human conditions in prisons and concentration camps, are deported, or sometimes vanish without trace.'

Transcaucasia
Georgia and Armenia appear to have stronger nationalist movements than Azerbaidzhan, where corruption is more of a problem for the regime.

Armenia is witnessing a combination of nationalist and religious opposition to CPSU ideology, in some ways resembling trends in Lithuania. Robert Nazaryan, sentenced in December 1978 to five years in labour camps plus two years internal exile, is a deacon of the Armenian Church. At his trial, 12 of the 13 witnesses testified in his favour, but he was nonetheless found guilty of 'anti-Soviet agitation and propaganda'. In 1974 11 young Armenians were given long terms in strict regime camps for being members of the National United Party of Armenia (NOP), whose programme demanded the reunification with Armenia of its former territories in Turkey and Azerbaidzhan and denounced the CPSU for following an 'imperialist and tsarist' nationality policy. The group produced the *samizdat* journals *Lighthouse* and *Efforts*, and issued a memorandum on its tenth anniversary in 1976.

The execution of Stepan Zatikyan and two other Armenians was announced in *Pravda* (31 January 1979); they had been accused of terrorism, causing an explosion in the Moscow underground and planning another bombing at the Kursk Railway Station in Moscow in 1977.

In *Georgia* on 8 February 1977, it was reported that Vladimir Zhvaniya had been sentenced to death for causing explosions outside public buildings in Sukhumi, Kutaisi and Tbilisi. In April 1978, after nationalist demonstrations against Russification, Georgian was reinstated in the republic's new constitution as the official language. In 1981 alone there were five separate demonstrations involving hundreds of people protesting against restrictions on the Georgian language and cultural heritage. The local Komsomol (Young Communist) First

Secretary demanded an 'uncompromising battle against dabbling in politics and playing at pseudo-nationalist heroics' (*Molodezh Gruzii* 12 December 1981).

Not all racial conflict in the USSR is directed against the Russians, however. In the Abkhazian ASSR the Abkhazians complained of mistreatment by the Georgians and vice versa. In the North Ossetian ASSR, clashes between Ossetians and Ingushi in October 1981 led to thousands of angry demonstrators occupying a government building and attacking police before tanks were brought in and the crowd dispersed with smoke bombs and tear gas.

Muslim republics

Less is known of nationalist resentments in the Muslim republics, although tensions certainly exist. The murders of KGB Lieutenant-General Arif Geidarov in Azerbaidzhan (June 1978) and of Sultan Ibraimov, Prime Minister of Kirgizia, in December 1980 have not been properly explained, although their deaths were announced in the official media. Some reports alleged that Muslim nationalists were responsible for Ibraimov's murder.

In January 1981, Azerbaidzhan First Secretary Geidar Aliev told a meeting of KGB officers in Baku that it was necessary to increase their vigilance in areas bordering on Islamic countries. The previous month the republic's KGB chief, Major-General Ziya Yusif-Zade, emphasised the need to resist chauvinism and 'national narrow-mindedness' and to counteract the activities of the 'sectarian underground and reactionary Muslim clergy' (*Bakinsky rabochy* 19 December 1980). In Turkmenistan, First Secretary Mukhamednazar Gapurov criticised party officials for seeming 'powerless in the ideological struggle against a small group of religious charlatans' (*Turkmenskaya iskra* 21 July 1979).

Concern at the resurgence of Islam in Iran and Afghanistan has made the Soviet authorities redouble their efforts against what they regard as 'superstition' and 'vestiges of the past' among Central Asian and Caucasian Muslims. Pilgrimages to shrines were mocked (*Turkmenskaya iskra* 1 September 1981), and the press repeatedly attacked the spreading of unregistered Muslim groups and the increase in clandestine mosques. In Turkmenistan, Kirgizia and Kazakhstan some party members were expelled for attending religious ceremonies. In Uzbekistan the party organ *Pravda vostoka* (10 October 1981) proclaimed that 'religion exaggerates and distorts the manifestation of nationalist feelings'.

Although colonised by the Russians in the 19th century, the Muslims of Central Asia have generally not been assimilated, and concern in Moscow is sharpened by the fact that the Muslim population's growth rate is much greater than that of the European nations of the USSR.

Thus in the 1980s Central Asians will account for 15 per cent of conscripts as compared with only some 7 per cent in the 1960s, and problems of integrating them into the armed forces will be even greater. If they are encouraged to move to the European areas because of growing labour shortages, race relations could become more strained than at present as they compete for housing and consumer goods.

Emigration

There are other smaller nations without union republic status which do not even have the theoretical right, supposedly 'guaranteed' in Article 72 of the Soviet constitution, that 'each Union Republic shall retain the right freely to secede from the USSR'. While they cannot be said to threaten the unity of the USSR, some have caused the Soviet authorities considerable trouble. There are would-be emigrants among Soviet nationalities other than the Jews, ethnic Germans and Armenians, but because of pressure from the United States and West Germany there have been more successful applications for exit visas among these nations. Israel, the USA and West Germany offer them a home while other Soviet peoples have nowhere to go.

By 1982 over 260,000 Jews, 70,000 Germans and 10,000 Armenians had left the USSR despite all the harassment by the authorities to which they exposed themselves. The flow appears to be influenced more by the state of Moscow's relations with Washington and Bonn and by the Soviet desire for Western technology than by the presence of applicants, and this has certainly damaged the image of the USSR in the world. Refusing visas tends to confirm accusations that the USSR is the 'prison of nations', while granting permission encourages others to apply and allows much negative information about the realities of life in the USSR to reach the rest of the world. The authorities may have hoped that emigration would rid them of dissident leaders; in fact it acquired a life of its own and became self-perpetuating, with recent emigrés inviting relations who remained to come and join them in the West.

Other national minorities

Minorities which lack powerful support abroad are less likely to achieve their aims. The Crimean Tatars, Meskhetians, Khemshins and other peoples exiled during the war to inhospitable parts of the USSR have been trying since their 'rehabilitation' by Khrushchev to return to their homelands. There have been several mass demonstrations by Crimean Tatars in Central Asia, and those who returned to the Crimea without official permission have been arrested and their homes confiscated or destroyed. *Samizdat* sources have reported cases of self-immolation by Crimean Tatars protesting against this treatment.

Religion

Clearly all religious believers dissent by definition from the atheist ideology of the ruling CPSU, but passive disagreement can become active opposition when the state takes steps to stamp out the 'opium of the masses'. Roman Catholicism in Lithuania, the Armenian and Georgian churches in Transcaucasia and Islam in Central Asia tend to combine with nationalism in alienating the populations from Moscow's policies. Acknowledging the strength of religious convictions even among the young and in the armed forces (see for example, *Krasnaya zvezda* 7 July 1982), the Soviet authorities have reached an uneasy compromise with the religious believers of the USSR – Christians, Muslims, Jews, Buddhists – allowing them to worship but forbidding them to proselytise, even in some extreme cases removing children from religious parents.

For most believers this compromise is not enough, and all the religions have their martyrs who have suffered persecution, imprisonment, even death in defence of their faith. The significance of this as a threat to the regime's stability is difficult to assess. Even Soviet sociologists in the official press tend to concede that the population of the USSR contains more convinced believers (20 per cent) than convinced atheists (15 per cent), but even if the proportion of believers is much higher, they are unlikely to challenge the political control of the CPSU. They are even less likely to support the regime, however, should it come under threat from some other source. Discrimination against believers, moreover, has led many young people to join the human rights movement in a more general struggle for social justice.

Human rights movement

The dissidents (*inakomyslyashchie*) who became famous in the world press in the late 1960s and 1970s fulfilled a major role in educating the West about the realities of life in the USSR at a time when détente fostered the illusion that the fundamental aims of Soviet strategy had somehow changed. By deliberately cultivating contacts with foreign correspondents in Moscow, they not only reached world public opinion, but also, through Radio Liberty, the BBC, Voice of America and other Western-financed radio stations, succeeded in disseminating their views throughout the USSR. This was furthered by the blossoming of *samizdat*, especially in the form of journals such as the *Chronicle of Current Events*, which first appeared in 1968 and has survived into the 1980s. The accuracy of its reports has been of a consistently high level.

When Brezhnev signed the Final Act of the Conference on Security and Cooperation in Europe (CSCE) at a meeting of high representatives from the countries of Europe, the USA and Canada held in Helsinki in August 1975, détente appeared to be strengthening the position of civil rights activists. To the United Nations Declaration on Human Rights and other such documents were added the principles of the Helsinki agreement, published in full in *Pravda* and *Izvestiya*. Groups 'to assist the implementation of the Helsinki accords' were set up in the next few years in Moscow, Lithuania, Ukraine, Georgia and Armenia. The members of these groups publicised violations of the Helsinki Final Act by the Soviet authorities, which reacted by arresting and imprisoning most of those responsible.

After the invasion of Afghanistan in December 1979 and the deterioration of East–West relations, the suppression of known dissidents proceeded apace despite the protests of world public opinion. In January 1980 the most prominent dissident, Academician Andrei Sakharov, who had sacrificed his comfortable position as a member of the Soviet élite to defend civil rights and publicise the plight of less well-known victims of the regime, was forcibly removed from Moscow and exiled in Gorky, a city closed to foreigners. Several other well-known dissidents, including Aleksandr Solzhenitsyn, had already been forced into exile in the West, and by 1982 hundreds of human rights activists had joined the thousands of political prisoners and religious believers serving their sentences in the harsh conditions of Soviet labour camps.

Opponents of the regime felt the need to reassess their position in view of the effectiveness of the KGB clampdown. Yet another turning point had been reached. After the 20th CPSU Congress in 1956 and the subsequent Khrushchev policy of de-Stalinisation, some party members supported the efforts of the liberal intelligentsia to democratise Soviet life. The movement to 'restore Leninist principles' in party life was centred on the literary circles around the journal *Novy mir*, edited by Aleksandr Tvardovsky. Many figures famous in the dissident movement such as Solzhenitsyn emerged at this time. Under Brezhnev a gradual policy of rehabilitating Stalin became evident and the shape of things to come was made clear by the show trial of Daniel and Sinyavsky in 1968. This was followed by a series of trials which almost appeared self-generating, since those who publicly protested at the gross abuse of the legal system themselves became the next victims.

The invasion of Czechoslovakia in 1968 called forth a brave but short-lived public protest in Red Square by a few young intellectuals who felt some sense of responsibility for their government's actions. The speed with which such demonstrations were crushed by the authorities might have made protest seem pointless were it not for the relaxation of East–West tension known as détente. Because the USSR needed advanced technology and know-how from the West, world public opinion was now of much greater importance to the Soviet leadership. By basing their dissent firmly on the Soviet constitution and on international agreements signed by the Soviet Union, the demo-cratic movement was able to make its voice heard at home and abroad. This caused the Soviet leadership considerable embarrassment during the delicate negotiations with the Western democracies for cheap credit and favourable technology import deals.

Any protection which East–West détente may have offered the dissi-dents was lost with the heightened tensions arising from disputes over Afghanistan, the Moscow Olympic Games and events in Poland. The authorities' tolerance of dissent, never great, gave way to a determina-tion, voiced by KGB leaders in their public statements, to eradicate all 'individual, anti-Soviet, nationalistic elements, politically unstable or morally decayed personages' (KGB First Deputy Chairman Semen Tsvigun, *Kommunist* no.14, 1981). For many liberal intellectuals the only possible way to reform the system was to work in secret, but there is no reason to see the human rights movement either as a failure or as something which has come to an end.

The publicity won by groups such as the Working Commission to Investigate the Use of Psychiatry for Political Purposes has been extremely important in putting pressure on the authorities to improve their treatment of individuals who have offended the regime. The civil rights movement, which covers a wide range of political convictions, from Marxists to liberals and Russian nationalists, and has united religious activists with campaigners for national minorities, has shown an extraordinary ability to survive, despite the imprisonment of many leading protesters. The dissidents show every sign of being determined to continue their works, with new members replacing those in prison.

(There are many good accounts in English of the human rights movement of the 1970s, some by exiled participants now continuing the struggle in the West. Several émigré publishing houses [such as Valery Chalidze's Khronika Press] have ensured the wider distribution of dissident views.)

Clandestine opposition

Nonetheless, in discussing the stability of the regime in the 1980s it may be more significant that a growing number of opposition groups have decided that working clandestinely can be more effective, while con-tinuing to circulate leaflets exposing the abuses of the authoritarian system. There are several interesting indications in *samizdat* of this trend, including the 'party programmes' of three political groupings which claim to have organised an underground struggle against the CPSU leadership.

The Initiative Group for National Democracy (IGND) points out, in a document drafted in July 1981, that the population of the USSR has no way of controlling the dangerously expansionist foreign policy and domestic repression of the regime, and that not even the 17 million members of the CPSU exert any political influence. Power is the preserve of the 'party oligarchy, numbering approximately 100,000 functionaries in party committees'. All major decisions are taken 'at the very top in a narrow circle of top party leaders'. The members of this party élite run the country in their own interests, guaranteeing a steady improvement in their privileges – special salaries, housing, shops, restaurants, holidays, priority in educational institutions, medical treatment, etc., but they have 'raised their own living standards by cruelly exploiting the rest of the population':

The social and economic consequences of these policies have been depressing: no-one in fact is prepared to answer for anything; technology stands idle, equipment breaks down, spare parts are stolen, houses deteriorate more quickly than they can be built. Thrift and care, rationalisation and inventiveness, initiative and innovation – everything is frozen and turned into fiction. Corruption and embezzlement have permeated the whole state system from top to bottom; economic crisis goes hand in hand with government chaos and a catastrophic fall in labour productivity and labour discipline.

According to the IGND the only way to change this disastrous situation is to penetrate the existing power structure and work in secret within the party, state and economic administration. Opposition groups should operate separately with the minimum of links, to reduce the threat from KGB informers. They must gather and disseminate information about the violation of civil rights, exploitation of the masses and élite privileges to win recruits and organise mass opposition. This would lead to widespread political action: distributing leaflets, initiating meetings, demonstrations and strikes.

The figure of the professional revolutionary will again appear in our public life; a convinced and decisive man of action who will gather around himself people ready to deny themselves material well-being and a normal family life, who will sacrifice their own freedom for the freedom and happiness of their people.

The aims of the IGND are set out in the document. They include the establishment of full political and civil rights in a multi-party parliamentary democracy; decentralisation with properly instituted local government; a federal system of national republics, each free to secede by referendum of all the population; a mixed economy, with some sectors of the economy vital for the defence of the country to be under state ownership, collective ownership for most branches of industry, and private ownership in agriculture and the service sector. There is no evidence about the strength of the IGND, but by calling themselves the 'Initiative Group' they suggest the beginning of a movement rather than a large organisation already in existence.

The memorandum of the Democratic National Front of the Soviet

Union (DNFSS) emphasises the danger of a nuclear holocaust being triggered by the foreign adventures of the Soviet regime and deplores the bloodshed in Afghanistan. It condemns also the mismanagement of domestic affairs:

And we, in our own country, are outraged by the state authorities, with their false promises, discriminatory laws and staged elections. Our civil rights are more restricted than before the October Revolution, more restricted than in any other country today. Our food supplies, services and consumer goods are the worst in the world – and they are sold at speculative prices. Our wages are lower than unemployment benefits in advanced countries. We are close to going hungry, in a land with the richest resources in the world. We have been brought to this by the inability of our leadership to look at the world in a realistic way, to recognise and face up to their responsibilities.

The Soviet leaders, claims the DNFSS, merely attempt to correct their own tragic mistakes without admitting that they are an 'everyday, integral part of their authoritarian system'. A proclamation issued by the DNFSS and circulated in Moscow, Leningrad and the Baltic States called for a strike on the first working day of each month, starting at 10 am, as a symbol of mass protest at the Soviet occupation of Afghanistan and interference in Poland. The proclamation demanded reform of the food distribution system and observance of human rights. The strikes began on 1 December 1981 and continued into 1982 without becoming widespread or general; several arrests were reported following clashes with the authorities over the stoppages suggesting some support for the DNFSS, since for every active member prepared to risk his or her freedom there are usually several dozen passive sympathisers.

The aims of a third group, the National Democratic Union (NDS) are stated in its programme as: 'democratising the country, developing scientific and cultural progress, re-establishing political and civil rights, liquidating bad management and raising the living standards of the Soviet people'. It intends to recruit its secret membership not only in factories, educational institutions and the armed forces, but also among party and government officials aware of the need for drastic changes.

This document was criticised both for its style and its contents in another *samizdat* publication, the *Information Bulletin* of the Free Interprofessional Association of Workers (SMOT), which since 1978 had been openly attempting to criticise and compensate for the lack of action by the official party-controlled trades unions on working and living conditions. Yet SMOT leaders too have suffered imprisonment and exile for working publicly to reform the system, according to Albina Yakoreva, expelled from the USSR in August 1982 for her work with the free trade union. Now this organisation has also decided to continue its activities underground.

Because of repression in Moscow and Leningrad, over 20 SMOT groups have been established to operate independently in the provinces, Ukraine and Baltic states. She said there were about 300 active members and 1,500 passive supporters. Earlier attempts to establish independent trades unions to fight for better working conditions were likewise subjected to determined KGB harassment, and leaders such as Vladimir Klebanov were imprisoned, or confined in psychiatric hospitals.

Worker discontent

The need for such unions is made clear not only in reliable *samizdat* publications, such as the SMOT *Information Bulletin* (of which 27 issues had appeared by January 1982), but also in the horrifying accounts published in *Trud* and other state newspapers of how workers complain in vain to their official unions and management about deplorable living conditions and the violation of labour safety codes. Is there a possibility that worker discontent could develop into a mass opposition movement threatening the stability of the regime in a way never envisaged by the hundreds of human rights activists?

There is some evidence that large-scale worker riots, as distinct from nationalist demonstrations, have taken place in the USSR. A mass strike (regarded under Soviet law as 'gross group violation of public order' or as 'mass disorders' and punishable by up to 15 years imprisonment or the death penalty) took place in August 1959 in Temirtau, Kazakhstan, and had to be suppressed by troops. Three men were shot for leading a riot in Vladimir oblast (*Vechernaya Moskva* 17 August 1961). Mass disorders were reported in 1962 in industrial towns in the southern RSFSR, with government buildings being attacked in Novocherkassk; hundreds were killed before the army restored order.

The disastrous harvest of 1963 brought 'violations of public order' in several major cities. In 1967 police stations were sacked in Chimkent, and three men were later tried and executed for 'outrages' (*Kazakhstanskaya pravda* 17 September 1967). In 1968 there were bread riots in Khorol near Vladivostok, where miners reportedly demonstrated with banners reading 'No bread – no work'. The riots in Dneprodzerzhinsk on 25 June 1972 are documented in some detail in *samizdat* sources, which state that some 10,000 people sacked police and party headquarters before troops could clear the streets. (The evidence for these riots, which can take years to reach the West, is discussed by Robert Conquest in 'Russian workers' riots', *Soviet Analyst*, vol. 2, no. 25, December 1973.)

More recently there have been reports of short strikes, usually limited to one or two factories, and speedily brought to an end by the authorities first agreeing to make some concessions and later arresting the ringleaders. Events in Poland were followed with considerable interest, and in a *samizdat* document a Russian worker, Nikolai Alekseev, while deploring the general passivity of Russians, emphasised that the Soviet leaders 'are afraid that if the workers of the USSR follow the Polish workers and refuse to cover up the utter bankruptcy of this system of lies and oppression by sacrificing their health, free time and whole way of life, then Soviet rule will collapse'.

The SMOT *Information Bulletin* covered Polish affairs is great detail and the 26th issue (December 1981–January 1982) is completely given over to 'Communist excesses on Polish soil'; issue no.27 devoted a further 16 closely typed pages to continuing this indignant, well-informed denunciation of martial law in Poland.

In the 1980s the greatest threat to the stability of the regime could come from a similar combination of nationalist, religious and worker discontent to that seen in Poland. An Estonian *samizdat* journal with the rather cumbersome title *Some Additions to the Free Flow of Ideas and News in Estonia* stated in issue no. 9 that a successful two-day strike for bonus payments in Tartu in October 1980 had taken place. The issue also included a telegram to Lech Walesa, dated 11 September 1980: 'We congratulate you and the Polish nation for laying the foundation of the democratic reforms that are so greatly needed by the whole socialist bloc.' It was signed by 20 Estonians and Lithuanians.

The regular reader of the Soviet press, however, finds so many examples of economic inefficiency, corruption in the administration and general lack of morality that he or she might well think that the system has already broken down. The regime appears to have no effective answer to economic inefficiency, and tries to deal with corruption by publicising draconian measures taken against some of the most guilty. Among the 30 or so executions for economic crimes which are reported most years in Soviet newspapers, there are some high ranking officials. For instance, the USSR Procurator General Aleksandr Rekunkov stated:

The special public danger posed by bribe takers makes it necessary to use against them the most severe measures of punishment. No leniency should be shown here. Former Deputy Minister of Fisheries Rytov, exposed as having committed such a crime, was sentenced by the USSR Supreme Court to an exceptional measure of punishment. The sentence has been carried out.

(*Pravda* 27 April 1982)

Vladimir Rytov appears to have been involved in a highly lucrative business smuggling caviar in tins marked smoked herring for sale in the West to earn hard currency for consumer goods unavailable in the Soviet Union. In another case, a chairman of a Tbilisi raion soviet (the local government in the area), Yura Kobakhidze, was executed for 'trading in state and co-operative apartments' (*Kommunisti* 3 August 1980), while in Azerbaidzhan, five factory and collective farm managers were sentenced to death for 'gross corruption' (*Bakinsky rabochy* 5 December 1975). For the most part, however, higher officials escape with a prison sentence, while ordinary bureaucrats convicted of embezzling similar amounts are shot.

The fact that these crimes are given publicity in the official media suggests that bribery, corruption and dishonesty have become a widespread answer to chronic shortages and low pay. Theft from the state is clearly not regarded as reprehensible in the way that stealing from an individual would be. The economy suffers also from absenteeism and drunkenness, again regular topics in the press. Cynics argue that workers who spend their time doing deals on the black market or drinking themselves into a stupor have no time for political activities against the regime, but while this may not be totally without foundation, the government clearly needs considerable improvements in labour productivity to ensure economic growth. Unless the economy improves to permit better food supplies and access to consumer goods, discontent will provide fertile ground for opponents of the regime to recruit support.

For the time being, the methods of control available to the leadership appear to be adequate. The most widespread method of controlling tensions is to encourage apathy and acceptance of the system among the population. Family and career pressures are such that most people prefer to conform rather than risk their children's careers in what must seem pointless resistance to oppression. Censorship, though breached to some extent by *samizdat*, *tamizdat* (materials published in Russian abroad and circulated in the USSR) and foreign broadcasts, is still effective in shaping the outlook of millions of Soviet citizens and makes it very difficult for opponents of the regime to co-ordinate their activities. This means that the organs of coercion – KGB and MVD militia – are able to deal with opposition piecemeal.

Controlling the population of the USSR is helped by the internal passport regulations whereby every Soviet citizen of 16 and over must be able to produce on request comprehensive personal documentation. It is still difficult for citizens to leave the area in which they are officially registered without the express permission of the authorities. The KGB has organised a widespread network of secret informers which enables the security organs to learn very quickly of most attempts to recruit for an opposition movement. Should an anti-regime demonstration get out of hand the Ministry of Internal Affairs (MVD) has a body of internal troops based in barracks in most large towns and equipped with tanks and armoured vehicles for controlling riots.

There are many potential causes of instability in the USSR today which bear some resemblance to the situation in the Russian empire before the revolution. It was not, however, until the third year of a disastrous world war that the tsarist system finally collapsed, and the Soviet regime likewise has a stability apparently based more on passive toleration than active support. Nonetheless, dangerous foreign adventures or a drastic deterioration in the country's economic situation could quickly change widespread discontent and grumbling into mass opposition.

4 Soviet Economic Prospects: Can the Soviet Economic System Survive?
Alan H. Smith

Self-sufficiency and survival

Economic self-sufficiency and economic survival are not, of course, the same thing. Economic activity, in the sense of the maintenance of the basic acts of production and consumption, must always 'survive' in any situation short of total devastation. The economist, who is mainly concerned with how efficiently economic activity is conducted and the level at which it takes places, would normally consider that an attempt to achieve self-sufficiency would hinder rather than help the efficient working of the economy.

The Soviet analyst however is frequently as much concerned with problems of 'political economy' as with the concept of economic efficiency and it is in this sense that economic self-sufficiency and economic survival may be considered to be complementary. First, economic systems are man- or woman-made and need not necessarily survive beyond the period of office of their creators. One may therefore ask whether the Soviet economic *system* can survive without substantial reform, and whether a future Soviet leadership may wish to change key features of the economic system. This question is linked to 'self-sufficiency' in that the endurance of the basically unreformed Stalinist economic system has depended to a considerable extent on Soviet self-sufficiency in natural resources. This has led many Western analysts to speculate what the effect would be on the Soviet economy and Soviet economic system if domestic demand for energy resources were to outgrow domestic supply.

Secondly, it has been argued that there are crucial areas in which the Soviet economy is dependent on imports, and in particular on imports from the West. This is most noticeable in the case of grain and other agricultural commodities, and in the 1970s has been extended to so-called 'high-technology' products. Consequently some observers in the West, and in particular in the USA, have perceived an area in which Western political goals could be achieved by exerting economic pressures. The basic policy of the Carter administration was not to attempt to bring about change in the economic system as such, but to pursue a policy of linkage, whereby trade would only be conducted if the USSR made certain *political* concessions, notably in the field of human rights. Following the Soviet invasion of Afghanistan the policy was extended to include an embargo on US exports of grain to the USSR (over and above those deliveries included in long-term contracts).

Western analysts have also argued that Soviet demand for imports from the West arises from systemic weaknesses in the operation of the unreformed economic system. This analysis leads to the view that the maintenance of East–West trade serves mainly to support the continued existence of the Soviet economic system, delays the process of economic reform and in turn strengthens the position of the hardline conservative factions in the Soviet leadership. It is also proposed that the reforms necessary to overcome these systemic weaknesses would have to provide a greater incentive to innovation at the enterprise level, which would in turn require greater access to accurate information and greater freedom to take independent decisions at all stages of the production process. Such economic reform, it is argued, would only be successful if accompanied by political changes which gave improved access to information to a larger section of the population and provided an environment which stimulated independent analysis. The logic of this argument, which has clearly been influential in shaping the policies of the Reagan administration, is that any form of East–West trade which reduces the need for domestic economic reform simultaneously delays the process of political reform.

A further corollary of this argument is that any trade that increases the productive capacity of the Soviet economy also increases the resources at the leadership's disposal for defence purposes, while imports of products which embody technology that cannot be produced domestically may also filter through to use in the defence sector.

Trade however benefits both partners, and both partners must therefore expect to suffer from its curtailment. The grain embargo was not without its effects on both the Soviet economy and the Soviet leadership and may have contributed to meat shortages in the USSR in the summer of 1980 (which resulted from the early slaughter of cattle due to insufficient feedstocks). Despite the Soviet leadership's perennial reluctance to give in openly to economic pressure and grant political concessions, the reforms in agricultural organisation announced in May 1982, which may involve the diversion of substantial resources towards agriculture, were perhaps engendered by the desire to avoid such pressure in the future.

However the American farming community also suffered considerably from the loss of markets and had to be subsidised by the US taxpayer, while much of the Soviet grain deficit was filled instead by imports from Canada, Australia and Argentina. This lack of unanimity and its cost to the USA caused the then presidential candidate Ronald Reagan to promise to end the embargo, a pledge which he honoured in April 1981, at a time when speculation in America that the Soviet Union would invade Poland was at its highest. At the same time (and long before the declaration of martial law in Poland) the Reagan administration put pressure on its European allies not to participate in the construction of a major gas pipeline from Urengoi in Western Siberia. This pipeline would eventually supply 40 billion cubic metres of natural gas to European Russia, Eastern Europe and ten West European countries and American anxieties centred largely on the prospect of West European countries (particularly West Germany) becoming so dependent on the USSR for energy supplies that their capacity for independent political action would be affected. West European leaders and officials have argued that this claim is exaggerated. Stern estimates that when the pipeline is operating at full capacity, Soviet supplies would account for about 35 per cent of the domestic consumption of natural gas in West Germany, Italy and France (much of which can be substituted at short notice by oil) and Soviet energy supplies would account for about 6 per cent of those countries' total energy consumption (Stern 1982: 68–73). Stern also argues that American estimates of the possibilities of increasing alternative secure energy sources for Western Europe (including nuclear power, US coal, US synfuels, and Algerian, Nigerian and Norwegian natural gas) are overoptimistic and that the failure to construct the Urengoi pipeline would lead to increased dependence on Middle Eastern oil (Stern 1982: 79–84). West European analysts tend to argue that the danger of disruption to energy supplies from political factors is greater in the Middle East, and that it is difficult to envisage a situation in which the West would cede to Soviet political pressure as a result of a threat to cut off 6 per cent of its energy supplies. It is also argued that the repercussions of such an action, which would greatly reduce the value of the pipeline itself to the USSR and would severely damage East–West trade in the future, would be greater for the USSR than for Western Europe.

In addition to providing alternative energy sources, the pipeline offers considerable opportunities to West European exporters. The principal beneficiaries will be the suppliers of large-diameter pipe, which will provide a welcome boost to the recession-hit steel industries of Western Europe. The other principal Western component will be the compressor stations, the majority of which are produced by companies in Italy, West Germany and the UK under licence from the General Electric Company based in the United States.

In response to this American pressure, the USSR announced in July 1982 that it would proceed with the construction of the pipeline using domestically produced compressor stations. The importance of the pipeline to the USSR is that sales of natural gas will enable it to maintain its hard currency earnings in the late 1980s, when it is anticipated that the volume of oil available for export to the West will decline. Therefore, the increased use of natural gas by Eastern Europe will help to preserve existing Soviet oil deposits and simultaneously reduce East European demand for imported oil from the West.

The construction of the pipeline has now become a major priority for Soviet industrial development involving questions of prestige. Its construction will require considerable expertise and labour skills, particularly to overcome climatic problems and will raise many questions that are central to Soviet economic development in the 1980s, including the question of economic self-sufficiency and survival. How dependent is the USSR on imported technology and can it, if required, produce the compressor stations domestically? (The situation was eased in November 1982 when the US government abandoned its opposition to Western firms participating in the project.) How dependent is it on energy exports for hard currency earnings and what is the importance of these earnings to the economy? Before answering these questions directly, it is necessary to examine the Soviet planning system and the current problems it faces.

Soviet economic development since the fall of Khrushchev
In 1961 Khrushchev made his famous pledge that the Soviet Union would overtake the USA in the per capita output of major items of production by 1980, and so win the war between communism and capitalism by means of peaceful competition. His claim was mainly based on the arithmetic extrapolation of the high rates of growth of industrial output that had been achieved in the late 1940s and 1950s which are shown in Table 4.1. It can also be seen from Table 4.1. row 5 that the rate of growth of industrial output has declined in each Five Year Plan since the war, culminating in a fairly modest rate of growth in 1976–80. Although it is planned that this decline should be reversed in 1981–5, the planned rate of growth of industrial output remains modest by pre-1975 Soviet standards.

Similarly the rate of growth of Net Material Product (the nearest Soviet equivalent to the Western concept of National Income, but which excludes the 'output' of services) has declined in each plan period since the war except 1966–70 (Table 4.1 row 1).

The decline in the rate of growth of output has been accompanied by a decline in the rate of growth of inputs, particularly to the industrial sector. The rate of growth of the industrial labour force (measured crudely as the number of workers and employees – Table 4.1 row 11) has declined since 1966, while the slowdown in the growth of industrial output in category A (production of the means of production – Table

Table 4.1   Indices of Soviet economic development 1950–85 (percentage growth rates pe Five Year Plan)

	1951–5	1956–60	1961–5	1966–70	1971–5	1976–80	Plan 1981–5
A. BASIC INDICES							
Net Material Product	71	55	37	44	32	23	18–20
Labour force	24	23	24	17	13	10	0–1[a]
Investment	78	85	36	44	40	29	12–15
National Income per head	57	42	27	38	26	19	16–18
B. INDUSTRY							
(i) Outputs							
Gross output	85	64	51	50	43	24	26–8
Group 'A'	91	71	58	51	46	26	26–8
Group 'B'	76	51	36	49	37	21	27–9
Fuel	63	45	35	30	31	16	15–20[a]
(ii) Inputs							
Investment	81	69	39	38	39	29	12–15
Gross fixed assets	74	71	69	52	51		
Labour force	24	19	21	16	8	8	2.4[a]
C. INCOME AND EXPENDITURE							
Average wage	12.5	12.5	18.5	27	19.5	16	13–16
Total wage payments	39	38	47	49	35	28	13–17[a]
Retail turnover	89	56	34	48	36	24	22–5

Sources   All figures derived from official Soviet statistics. Plan data for 1981–5, and figures fo 1976–80 taken from *Pravda* 2 December 1980, and N.A. Tikhonov's speech to the 26t CPSU Congress, *Pravda* 27 February 1981.

Notes   [a] = own extrapolation
Industry: Industrial output is divided into two groups: group A – investment goods; an group B – consumption goods. Labour force is measured in average number of worker and employees. Average wage: average monthly wage. Retail turnover: value of sales i state retail stores. Official estimates of price changes in these stores are negligible.

4.1 row 6) has in turn resulted in a decline in the rate of growth of industrial investment. Finally this has resulted in a slowdown in the growth of industrial fixed assets – the basic source of Soviet economic growth.

It is frequently argued that a decline in the growth (or even the absolute level) of the population and the labour force will not affect per-capita living standards and will not therefore be a cause for concern to the Soviet leadership. There are however some exceptions to this in the Soviet case. Firstly, the per capita cost of certain collective or national goals (including defence, the space programme, aid to Third World countries, etc.) is of course related to the size of the population. Clearly it helps a superpower to have a large labour force; however, a growing labour force also helps to maintain a superpower. If a decline in the labour force is accompanied by a proportional decline in output growth, either the growth of defence expenditure must similarly decline or such items must utilise a larger proportion of national income. This will in turn affect the resources available for consumption, while more capital investment will be required to 'substitute' for labour. Secondly, for reasons examined below, the Soviet economic model tends to place greater emphasis on the growth of inputs as a source of economic growth and this factor also affects the growth of family incomes.

Furthermore, when the population is growing the inevitable per capita decline in demand for certain goods and services may be entirely or partially offset by the demands of an increased number of consumers. When the population ceases to grow this will no longer be the case and the demand for the outputs of entire plants may disappear. This will then require a painful adjustment process involving the prospect of open unemployment, which the Soviet economy has so far managed to avoid to any substantial degree.

Finally, however, most analyses of Soviet economic development indicate that the growth of inputs to industry has not matched in recent years the former growth of output, and as a result the rate of growth of industrial output has declined more sharply than the rate of growth of inputs. All these factors are reflected in the decline in the growth of National Income per head (Table 4.1 row 4) in each Five Year Plan period since the war except 1966–70, and by the estimates that show that only in the period 1951–5 did the growth of industrial output exceed the growth of industrial fixed assets.

Why has this pattern developed? The high growth rates recorded in the late 1940s and early 1950s can partly be explained by the 'catch-up phenomenon' of 'lost' economic growth resulting from the war, as the Soviet economy was both ravaged by wholesale destruction and partly isolated from technological developments and improvements that were taking place elsewhere in the world (see Gomulka 1976). The reconstruction of major industries in peacetime embodying these technological improvements therefore offered opportunities for high rates of growth of industrial output that could not be sustained in the long run. Once the 'stock' of technical developments and the scope for reconstruction has been assimilated, a more normal growth pattern was resumed.

The traditional Stalinist pattern of industrial growth placed greater emphasis on mobilising resources to achieve a high rate of growth of inputs to industry (extensive growth) than on improving the efficiency of existing inputs (intensive growth). During the Stalin years, high rates of industrial growth were achieved by devoting a relatively large proportion of National Income to investment and concentrating industrial investment in production of 'the means of production' which was defined by Stalin to embrace heavy industry – machinery, iron and steel, coal, and the like (see Fallenbuchl 1970). The pattern of extensive growth also placed emphasis on the construction of new plant, which was staffed by additions to the industrial labour force who came from the 'surplus labour' in agriculture (whose marginal productivity was considered to be low or zero) and by increased female participation in the labour force.

This pattern of growth has considerable limitations as a permanent model and was indeed slowing down on the eve of the Second World War. First, as the potential for the transfer of labour from agriculture to industry and urban participation rates in the labour force reach their natural limits, the growth rate of the industrial labour force will depend purely on demographic factors and will start to decline. Second, as the model places far greater emphasis on reinvestment from economic growth than on consumption, the major source of growth of family incomes arises from increased participation in the labour force and the growth of wage rates is lower than the growth of total family incomes. Consequently as the source of increased participation in the labour force dries up, more families find themselves forced to rely on the growth of individual wage rates as the source of family income growth.

Third, unless sufficient resources are devoted to developing the mineral and extractive industries and geological prospecting, the rapid growth of industrial production will put strain on domestic natural resources. Fourth, one would anticipate that the most accessible natural resources and the best located industrial sites would be the first to be developed, consequently the continuation of extensive growth requires that less preferred locations must be developed, leading to increased construction and transportation costs, etc. Consequently, a given unit of capital investment will achieve a lower return in the form of final output.

These macroeconomic problems are compounded by a further set of microeconomic problems arising from the nature of the Soviet planning system. Although the achievements of Soviet scientists and the Soviet record of production in prestige projects, such as the space programme, and many other large-scale construction projects command and deserve respect, the quality of this work does not permeate sufficiently through to the day-to-day operation of the economy. Indeed, the system of planning by priorities means that prestige sectors receive precedence in obtaining scarce resources (including skilled labour) over other sectors, while even within a given enterprise, managers will concentrate their attention on production, which they know party authorities consider important, to the detriment of other outputs. The industrial areas that will probably concern the Soviet leadership most in the 1980s (and which received considerable attention from Aleksei Kosygin, but to little avail) were the evidence of bias against innovation at the enterprise level, the high level of consumption of raw materials (particularly energy) per unit of output, and the question of whether the Soviet economy can produce an adequate range and style of consumer goods to satisfy its population.

The Soviet planning system is a hierarchical chain of command through which enterprises pass information about their production potential to superior agencies (industrial ministries or ministerial sub-departments known as *glavki*) who in turn aggregate this information and pass it up to the Central Planning Agency (Gosplan). Gosplan processes this information and passes a series of instructions and orders back down the hierarchy until they are eventually received by the enterprise in the form of binding plan instructions. These instructions specify in considerable detail what the enterprise is to produce and with what inputs, from where it is to receive these inputs, the size of its labour force and wage payments, new capital construction, etc. Unless the plan is perfectly accurate (a virtual impossibility in the real world) fulfilment of one instruction may require the violation of another. Planners give an indication to enterprises of the targets they consider to be the most important by paying money bonuses to managers and workers for the fulfilment and overfulfilment of those specific targets.

Enterprises, however, can influence the targets they receive (and thus their bonuses) by the information that they provide to central authorities. The central authorities are aware of this, and in attempting to coax an improved performance from the enterprise, normally establish plan targets which are based on the previous period's performance plus a certain percentage increase – the ratchet principle (see Birman 1978).

The vertical chain of command also means that enterprises are not in direct contact with the end-users of their products or the suppliers of their inputs, but produce according to central instructions. They are therefore more concerned with fulfilling the letter of the plan rather than the spirit of the plan.

During the Stalin era and much of the Khrushchev period, priority was mainly attached to the fulfilment and overfulfilment of gross output targets specified in physical units which resulted in a number of well-chronicled abuses. If output targets were specified in units of weight, enterprises had an incentive to produce fewer but larger units (e.g. large pre-cast concrete slabs) or if specified in volume a large number of small items (e.g. number of nails) and to produce commodities with few technical or stylistic variations, etc. Most critically, however, when enterprises concentrate purely on output targets, they tend to regard their inputs as 'costless' and over-indent for material supplies, capital construction, etc. A chronic sellers' market therefore arose in which enterprises were willing to accept virtually whatever inputs they were allocated because it *might* help them to achieve their targets (or be illegally bartered for something more useful) and as a result also had little regard for the quality or technical specifications of their outputs. This factor applies to both intermediate goods and consumer goods.

The planning system also works against innovation at the enterprise level, particularly in the production of 'new' products and, perhaps surprisingly, in the diffusion of new technology throughout the economy.

An innovating enterprise is effectively attempting to achieve something it has not been instructed to do. Even if it wins the approval of superior authorities for the innovation, it may require new inputs not specified in the plan, and it may incur initial problems of 'debugging' new processes. All of these will involve additional work for the enterprise and superior authorities, and may cause them to fail to fulfil their output targets and thus lose bonuses. Once the innovation has been carried out and is operating smoothly however, the 'ratchet' principle ensures that output targets will be revised upwards. Consequently the innovating enterprise tends to bear the initial costs of an innovation, but does not receive the long term benefits.

One would anticipate that, once an initial innovation has been achieved, it would be rapidly dispersed through the economy by the system of plan instructions. Empirical evidence, however, suggests that the reverse is true, and that the Soviet economy is exceedingly slow at diffusing new production processes. The explanation for this appears to be in part bureaucratic inertia, but mainly the genuine desire to maintain full employment levels, even to the extent of avoiding what is referred to in the West as 'frictional unemployment', resulting from changes in demand on the skill structure and location of the labour force.

The desire to maintain full employment, particularly while the labour force was expanding, resulted in a marked reluctance to close down or re-equip enterprises that were using older technology or producing commodities no longer in demand. As the growth of the labour force has slowed down, greater emphasis has had to be placed on manning new plants by offering alternative work to those who have been displaced by new innovations than by recruiting additional workers to the labour force. In many cases, the same ministerial authorities who are responsible for diffusing new production processes are also responsible for finding alternative employment, re-equipping and retraining workers. As a result, therefore, they also bear the costs of innovation but do not reap the rewards.

Schumpeterian theories of innovation suggest that the reverse is true in a capitalist economy. As a result of new innovations (e.g. micro-electronics) innovating firms make additional profits, while those who fail to innovate or produce commodities that are no longer in demand eventually go out of business. Firms are forced to keep abreast of new developments to preserve their competitive position, and as a result, new innovations are diffused throughout the economy relatively quickly. Effectively the innovator reaps the rewards and those who fail to innovate, and their employees, bear the costs. This process has been summed up by one Soviet economist as follows:

No Western employer can afford to lag behind in science and technology. Lagging behind spells death to the capitalist. But in capitalist society, while advanced technology brings higher profits to the employer it brings grief, poverty and unemployment to millions of people.

(Danilov 1981: 18)

It should be remembered that as much of this Western innovation is economic or cost-cutting in nature as is directed at producing technic-ally 'superior' products. A plastic bag may not be inherently superior to a leather case but it may perform the same functions at a far lower cost.

I once met an American engineer who had visited many Soviet enterprises on a number of business trips, and who spoke with undisguised pleasure at the technical quality of some of the machinery and engineering he had seen which was no longer used in the USA. He was aware that his was almost the enthusiasm of a railway or canal buff and concluded: 'Of course, in the States we just couldn't afford it'. It is intriguing that the principal sector in which technological deter-minism, dictated by government demands, frequently outweighs questions of cost-effectiveness, is the defence sector. There, only the most modern machinery must be used.

A critical problem for the Soviet leadership in the 1980s will be whether they can still 'afford' to maintain their high rates of consump-tion of raw materials, and if not, whether the diffusion of new technical processes can be combined with low levels of frictional unemployment, particularly as the possibility of manning new plants by additions to the labour force reduces further.

In the period since the ousting of Khrushchev, the Soviet leadership undertook one major internal and one external policy initiative in an attempt to overcome these problems. These policies are largely identi-fied with the person of Kosygin although there had been considerable debate on the need for domestic reform in party, government and academic circles during the Khrushchev era (see Lewin 1975: especially chapter 7). It had not escaped the attention of Soviet economists that economic growth in Western Europe had been largely based on increases in factor productivity rather than increases in total factor inputs. Those who proposed economic reform in the Soviet Union and Eastern Europe frequently justified their arguments by the need to shift from extensive to intensive growth, by utilising capital and labour inputs more effectively.

Domestic economic reforms, which were first announced by Kosygin in October 1965, were in principle to give more power to enterprise managers. The effect of the 1965 reforms and subsequent modifications, including two reform amendments in 1973 and 1979, was to alter the structure of the administration of the economy and to make some rational responses to certain specific problems, while leaving the basic economic system fundamentally unaltered.

Clearly any discussion of changes spread over 15 years in a country as large as the USSR, which contains some 49,000 enterprises producing some 4 million products, is a considerable abstraction and simplification, but some basic features can be identified. The most complicated organisational change was the creation of large economic units through the amalgamation of enterprises into 'production' or 'industrial' associations, whose effect was probably to give greater decision-making powers to a 'middle tier' of management at the expense of both central agencies and local enterprise managers.

Enterprises and production associations still received basic instructions concerning, for example, their output targets and the sources of their inputs, the size of the total wage fund, although the degree of detail contained under each heading was reduced. Enterprises were also to be encouraged to make more direct links with supplying enterprises to iron out such specific details as the timing and specification of deliveries, a task that was facilitated when co-operating enterprises came within the same association.

The most significant changes were in the structure of bonus-forming indices, which were to be based on monetary aggregates composed of a profit-rate (a percentage obtained by dividing enterprise revenue, minus operating and input costs, by fixed and working capital) and a percentage change in sales over a base period. The resulting percentages were then to be multiplied by norms – determined by the individual ministry – and by the total wage fund, to arrive at the size of available money bonuses (see Ellman 1969). By introducing input and capital costs directly into the bonus-forming indices, enterprises were to be provided with an incentive to reduce production costs. Subsequent amendments included permitting enterprises which economised on labour to pay out bonuses calculated on the basis of the original, not the reduced, wage fund.

The limitations of the reform process can be illustrated by the lack of autonomy granted to enterprises for any radical changes to their input and output plans. If central planners determine the output structure of an enterprise, and those outputs are another enterprise's inputs, enterprises cannot make spontaneous changes to their methods of production which require a change of inputs (e.g. substituting plastics for steel). Consequently it appears that decentralisation was chiefly intended to give enterprises an incentive to cut back on their consumption of inputs per unit of output rather than to permit them to make 'economic' decisions involving substitution of one input by another. Certainly enterprises are not encouraged to make changes in their production patterns which may have 'external' effects on the production patterns of other enterprises.

It is too early to say whether proposals announced in July 1979, which give enterprises greater power to draw up their own production plans, provided they are co-ordinated with supplying and receiving enterprises, will overcome this problem (Nove 1981). The fact that such plans should be stable for five years ahead, while helping to free enterprises from central interference, may inhibit spontaneous responses to changing circumstances.

A second major factor contributing to economic growth in Western Europe since the war has been the international transfer of technology. Information concerning new developments and production processes in one country (frequently, but not always, the USA) have been transferred to other countries by a variety of processes including technical journals, scientific conferences, discussion and casual (and not so casual) observation. The mere knowledge that a solution has been found to a problem provides a considerable impetus to the solution of that problem elsewhere.

In addition to such 'disembodied' technical transfers, technology may also be transferred by 'embodiment' in imports of machinery and equipment, as well as by the purchase of patents, licences, hiring of engineers and management specialists, etc. (Hanson 1981). Sutton has shown that the USSR actively used these techniques to acquire international technology during the 1930s (Sutton 1968–71). Many Western economists have argued that a major source of such international technology transfer since the war has been the activity of multi-national corporations (MNCs) seeking new markets or cheaper sources of labour. The USSR, which has not permitted overseas equity investment in its economy since the concession policies of the 1920s, found itself largely isolated from this form of technology transfer. Kosygin's major external initiative (accompanied by the political process of détente) was to stimulate greater cooperation with MNCs. In the case of MNC equity investment in a capitalist country, it is frequently the MNC itself which both raises or supplies the venture capital and bears the risk of the venture, taking the profits if it succeeds and the losses if it fails. In addition, it seeks the markets for the outputs of the venture or integrates the plant into its corporate supply structure.

The USSR and some other East European countries were unwilling to allow foreign ownership of capital in their economies and instead engaged, in the late 1960s and 1970s, in so-called co-operation ventures, involving the purchase of machinery and equipment, licences, facilities and the like from the West. The amount of expenditure required exceeded those countries' hard currency reserves, and the operation was largely financed by borrowing from Western banks with the intention of repaying the loans from the sale of the outputs of the newly-constructed plants in Western markets.

It is at this stage that the crucial differences between the Soviet economy and the East European economies indicated in Philip Hanson's paper in this volume arise, resulting from the former's endowment of natural resources, which require us to re-examine the question of self-sufficiency and the survival of economic systems.

The increase in world oil prices in 1974 resulted in a massive transfer of wealth from the industrial oil-consuming countries to the oil-producing countries. The latter however were not in a position to absorb the quantity of commodities such wealth could purchase and which industrial nations wished to produce. This in turn provoked a recession in the West while the oil producers simply lent their newly-acquired wealth to Western banks. Consequently, the energy crisis created finance-seeking (petrocurrencies) borrowers and Western producers seeking markets, just at the time when the Soviet Union and East Europe were seeking to acquire Western commodities on credit. This led to a short-term harmony between the economic interests of the East and the West, as Western banks lent hard currency to East European countries for the purchase of Western machinery and equipment. Many Western lenders who may have doubted the (hard currency) viability of the projects they were financing, comforted themselves with the 'umbrella theory', which argues that the USSR could and would stand the strain of Soviet and East European indebtedness by the sale of its increasingly valuable natural resources.

Holzman has argued that the East European failure to sell the output of their new plants to the West (outlined in Philip Hanson's paper) was the result not just of Western recession, but of the systemic planning problems, referred to above, which produced low quality outputs, a lack of responsiveness to changes in demand and so on (Holzman 1979). This hypothesis indicates that the policies of domestic reform of the economic system and importing technology are complementary – in order to pay for capital imports in the long run, it will be necessary for centrally-planned economies to make the economic system more responsive to Western market needs. It should not be concluded that reform always provides a perfect panacea to balance of payments difficulties – Hungary, the most decentralised economy, is also encountering fairly severe balance of payments problems. In the case of the Soviet Union, however, the abundance of natural resources has reduced the need to sell industrial products in the West, and so reduced the pressure for domestic reform on this account. Consequently, it is not just self-sufficiency, but surplus of raw materials that has helped to preserve the economic system.

Prospects for the 1980s

Although no substantial change of the economic *system* has been enacted since the ousting of Khrushchev, Soviet economic *policies* have shown some capacity for change. The most significant *policy* change has been the import of Western technology. The ability of the economic system to absorb this policy has, however, depended to a considerable degree on geographic factors. The sheer size of the Soviet Union and the consequent lower dependence on foreign trade has meant that large-scale turnkey projects have been absorbed in the economy without creating large-scale external effects. Soviet abundance in natural resources – oil, gas, gold, diamonds and non-ferrous metals – and the improved terms of trade resulting from price increases for those commodities strengthened the USSR's external position in the 1970s. Arms sales for hard currency also appear to have kept pace with Soviet imports of Western machinery (Smith 1982).

We should also be very wary of overestimating Soviet dependence on imported machinery – Philip Hanson has estimated that Western machinery and equipment make a contribution of about 0.5 per cent per annum to Soviet growth rates (Hanson 1981) and his paper in this volume indicates declining Soviet interest in Western technology in many areas in the second half of the 1970s.

Although Khrushchev's boast of overtaking the USA has not been realised, and it is extremely unlikely that it would have been realised even with a substantial economic reform, some considerable *quantitative* improvements to Soviet living standards have been made. Soviet statistics put Soviet Net Material Product at 67 per cent of that of the USA in 1979 and industrial output at 80 per cent. These figures must be further deflated to arrive at a per capita figure. Table 4.2 (based on official Soviet statistics) shows that nearly one in four of the Soviet population (approximately one per household) possessed a refrigerator, washing machine and TV set in 1979. Production of these items levelled out in the 1970s possibly indicating a degree of market saturation. This advance, though considerable, does not compare favourably with other East European countries. Ownership of the durables mentioned above is lower than in all East European countries except Bulgaria. A comparison of the growth of real per capita consumption in the Soviet Union and Eastern Europe since 1960 (based on official statistics) shows that Soviet growth rates are marginally higher than those of the GDR and Czechoslovakia (basically industrial nations), marginally lower than those of Poland and Hungary, and substantially below those of Bulgaria and Romania. On the assumption that the growth rate of consumption is inversely related to absolute consumption levels, the USSR should be placed higher than Hungary or Poland, at or about the level of Bulgaria. The explanation for this poorer relative performance must await further research but one possibility is the higher proportion of investment that produces no material return (defence and aid to Third World countries) and the diseconomies of scale arising from Soviet geography, including the need to transport raw material over vast distances and the increased cost of raising living standards of dispersed rural communities.

The basic quantitative data do not indicate the quality, style or efficiency of Soviet consumption items, and Brezhnev indicated before his death that this was a further item of concern. The per capita production and consumption of basic foodstuffs is still substantially below the East European average which indicates that agriculture is still the Achilles heel of the Soviet economy.

Further problems in the field of consumption and the provision of services are reflected in reports of the growth of legal and illegal market activities, queues, shortages of basic items at prevailing prices in state stores and the growth of household savings both in State Savings Banks and private currency hoards. Western analysts have debated whether these phenomena arise from microeconomic problems which cause Soviet consumers to prefer to save their money rather than spend it on what is currently available (e.g. poor quality outputs, irrational relative prices) or whether they result from repressed inflation (excess demand for the products in state stores in aggregate at current wages and prices). Birman, a proponent of the second school, has estimated that at the end of 1976, the total stock of household savings would have been sufficient to purchase 80 per cent of total sales in state retail stores (Birman 1980). Even if one accepts that these savings were initially voluntary, an expanded provision of consumer goods will be required to meet this deferred demand and to head off financial problems.

This problem is exacerbated by the general slowdown in growth rates. Consequently although the production of industrial consumer goods (Group A) is planned to grow faster than the production of

Table 4.2 Production and consumption of industrial products

	1950	1955	1960	1965	1970	1975	1980	Plan 1985
A. INDUSTRIAL PRODUCTS (million tonnes)								
Steel	27	45	65	91	116	141	148	
Iron ore	40	72	106	153	197	235		
Pig iron	19	33	47	66	86	103	107	
Electric energy (billion Kwh)	91	170	292	507	741	1039	1295	1550–1600
Coal	261		510	578	624	701	716	770–800
Natural Gas (billion m³)	5	8	42	119	185	270	435	600–640
Oil	38	71	148	242	353	491	603	620–645
Cement	10	22	45	72	95	122	124	140–42
Mineral fertilisers	1.2	2.3	3.3	7.4	13.1	22.0	24.8	36–7
Plastics & synthetic resins	0.07	0.2	0.3	0.7	1.7	2.8	3.64	6–6.25
Chemical fibres (thousand tonnes)	24	110	211	407	623	955	1176	1600
B. INDUSTRIAL CONSUMER GOODS (millions)								
Passenger cars	0.07	0.11	0.14	0.20	0.34	1.20	1.33	
Radios	1.1	3.5	4.2	5.2	7.8	8.4	8.5[a]	
Television sets	—	0.5	1.7	3.7	6.7	7.0	7.3[a]	
Washing machines	—	0.1	0.9	3.4	5.2	3.3	3.7[a]	
Refrigerators	—	0.2	0.5	1.7	4.1	5.6	6.0[a]	

a = 1979

C. PER CAPITA CONSUMPTION OF FOOD PRODUCTS (kilograms)

	1960	1965	1970	1975	1979
Meat and meat products	40	41	48	57	58
Fish and fish products	10	13	15	17	16
Milk and milk products	240	251	307	316	319
Eggs (no.)	118	124	159	216	233
Bread and flour	164	156	149	141	139
Fresh vegetables	70	72	82	89	95
Potatoes	143	142	130	120	119

D. OWNERSHIP OF CONSUMER DURABLES (per 1000 population)

	1960	1965	1970	1975	1979
Refrigerators	10		89	178	240
Washing machines	13		141	189	205
TV sets	22	68	143	215	242
Radios	129	165	199	230	246

Sources All figures derived from official Soviet statistics and Plan data.

investment goods (for the first time, if achieved) in the 1981-5 Five Year Plan, this involves reversing the downward trend in industrial growth rates. Even if this target is achieved, the volume of retail turnover in state stores will only grow at the, comparatively low, rate achieved in 1976-80 (see Table 4.1).

Demographic factors will also exercise a considerable influence on the growth rates of both industrial output and family income and consumption over the next decade. The size of the available labour force will be largely determined by the low birthrates recorded in the 1960s and the 1970s, and the USSR will inevitably be faced with an ageing population in the 1980s, which will probably result in problems of labour mobility, and, unless an increasing proportion of old-age people continue in employment, the prospect of a declining labour force.

Soviet authorities have already recognised that a smaller number of active people will be called upon to support a larger number of older citizens who will require increased resource expenditure on health and welfare provision and financial provision in the form of pensions. Furthermore, the vast majority of the population will have to depend on the growth of wage rates as the sole source of family income growth, as the growth of family incomes brought about by increased participation rates will cease. Indeed, many families, where older members leave the labour force, will find that family income will decline. There is some evidence that this phenomenon has been accompanied in Eastern Europe by increasing wage rate growth resulting in inflationary pressures. As wage-rates are only planned to grow 13-16 per cent over the next five years, this figure will reflect the most common rate of family income growth, although certain social security payments, including maternity and child benefits, are planned to grow somewhat faster, and wages and benefits to the lower-paid pensioners and collective farm workers are planned to grow more quickly than average incomes.

A more critical problem will be the geographic distribution of the population. The major areas of growth of the working-age population in the 1980s will be the rural districts of Central Asia and Kazakhstan, while Soviet economic development plans in the next decade are highly dependent on the development of West Siberian energy sources. The prospects of a substantial exodus of the population from the warmer climes of Central Asia to the harsher climes of Siberia, where an increase in income of at least 50 per cent would be necessary purely to compensate for heating, clothing, fresh food, and the like are not high. Furthermore, the possibility of overcoming the problem by immigration is limited although there are current reports that Cuban and Vietnamese workers are being encouraged to work in Siberia.

Ironically the problem of labour shortage may mean that is harder, not easier, to maintain the goal of full employment. As expanding areas of the economy cannot be staffed by an expanding labour force, increased emphasis will have to be placed on transferring workers from existing employment. The cost of maintaining labour in jobs that are no longer fully productive (disguised unemployment) will increase, and planners will be under increasing pressure to reduce manning levels and close down obsolete plants. Nikolai Tikhonov, the Prime Minister argued in his speech to the 26th CPSU Congress that mechanisation will replace 1.5 to 2 million jobs in the period up to 1985. Unless draconian measures for labour direction are introduced, frictional unemployment is likely to increase as the demands of the expanding areas for labour are not precisely matched by the skill structures and age rates of those in declining demand elsewhere. This has been recognised recently by Soviet manpower planners who argue that 'in individual cases employed workers may become redundant' (Breyev 1979: 15).

The question of the development of Siberian natural resources brings us back full circle to the question of 'self-sufficiency', and the question of the Urengoi pipeline. A much publicised CIA report, first published in 1977, predicted that the USSR and Eastern Europe combined would be net importers of crude oil amounting to 175–225 million tonnes by 1985 (which would cost 50 billion US dollars per annum at a price of 34 dollars a barrel). The CIA prediction was based on an assessment that Soviet production would fall by about 25 per cent to 450 million tonnes per annum while Soviet and East European demand would continue to grow at about 10 per cent per annum. In practice this estimate of Soviet production has proved to be very pessimistic, while the *growth* of consumption has also declined. In 1980 Soviet production was 603 million tonnes (against a plan target of 640 million tonnes), domestic consumption was around 440 million tonnes, 80 million tonnes was exported to Eastern Europe, 20 million tonnes to other socialist countries and about 55 million tonnes of oil and oil products were exported to the West. The total value of oil sales to the West was approximately 12 billion US dollars. Soviet planned production levels of 640 million tonnes for 1985 are considered by many Western analysts to be over-optimistic. Consequently, small changes in the estimation of the rate of growth of demand and the rate of decline or growth of supply have a significant effect on the total CMEA oil balance.

It is important under these circumstances to make two critical distinctions. Firstly, one must distinguish between the total CMEA position (which may be further subdivided to exclude Romania and the non-European CMEA nations) and the Soviet position alone. Secondly, one must distinguish between oil supplies and total energy supplies. Most estimates predict that the Soviet Union will remain a substantial net exporter of energy throughout the 1980s, but that natural gas will play an increasing part in this balance, and that net Soviet energy exports in terms of oil equivalent in 1990 will be below the 1980 levels (Scanlan 1981).

The position of the East European countries, particularly with respect to oil supplies, is more precarious. It is highly probable that total consumption of the Soviet Union and other socialist countries will exceed available supply by the latter half of the 1980s, if current growth rates of demand are maintained and unless there is substantial conversion of electricity production from oil to natural gas. The Urengoi pipeline will therefore play a critical role both in maintaining the CMEA energy balance by supplying Eastern Europe and in helping to maintain Soviet hard currency earnings.

The question of whether the West *should* assist in the construction of the pipeline is mainly political, but certain economic factors must be considered in attempting to answer it. Firstly – could the USSR construct the pipeline without Western assistance and what impact would this have on the rest of the economy? There is an abundance of Western anecdotal evidence to indicate Soviet inefficiency in the oil and gas industry. However, this is rapidly becoming a major priority sector and the evidence of Soviet successes in areas that have received priority treatment in general, and in pipeline construction in particular (sometimes involving continuous welding at temperatures of minus 20° C), should not be dismissed.

The major Western components are large diameter pipe and compressor stations. Although the USSR has not been particularly successful in producing the quality of steel required for large diameter pipe, the principal reasons for relying on imports are largely economic – it is just not worth expanding domestic production capacity for steel when substantial excess capacity exists in Western Europe (Stern 1982: 73–9). It is more tempting to see the failure to produce compressor stations as a sign of 'technological inability'. Economic factors, however, also play a considerable role. The fact that West European producers have chosen to buy licences for the production of compressor stations on the basis of US patents rather than develop the technology themselves makes it difficult to ascribe the failure to produce such items in the USSR purely to a 'systemic inability'. In effect the USSR is seeking to imitate Western Europe. Some Western analysts therefore feel that the Soviet claim that they could produce the compressor stations domestically is not unfounded.

The other major benefit to the USSR of Western participation in the pipeline project is the hard currency earnings resulting from the export of natural gas. It is in this area that the implications for Eastern Europe and in particular the 'Soviet umbrella theory' must be examined. In the late 1970s the USSR displayed a diminishing interest in acquiring

Western technology, and with some shift in domestic priorities could probably continue to export sufficient quantities of gold, diamonds, non-ferrous metals and arms to pay for imports of grain, foodstuffs and possibly even some quantities of higher quality consumer goods. These exports would also provide an incentive for labour mobility which could be priced at such levels as to mop up excess demand. Some degree of open inflation and unemployment may have to be countenanced but the economic *system* could survive, albeit with changes in policies.

Once the 'costs of empire' are taken into consideration, the picture becomes far less optimistic. Vital resources that could earn hard currency may have to be diverted to Eastern Europe, while additional investment in West Siberia may be necessary to maintain the physical volume of supplies. The scale as well as the quality of this effort may require Western co-operation.

If the Soviet Union is unable to substitute exports of natural gas for oil, or to convert a substantial volume of domestic and East European consumption from oil to natural gas, it is unlikely to be able to expand its other traditional exports in sufficient quantities to maintain the required volume of hard currency earnings to support Eastern Europe. Soviet gold production (approximately 300 tons per annum) and stocks (1500 tons) would be insufficient to finance or even pay off the Polish debt at a price of 400 US dollars an ounce. Financing total East European indebtedness would surely be beyond Soviet capabilities, even if they wished it. A time would come when the Soviet leadership would have to examine the advantages to it of assisting East European countries to pay off interest charges of 18–20 per cent without attempting to eliminate the total debt. With Western banks reluctant to make further loans to Eastern Europe, the effect of Soviet policy is the maintenance, at a considerable real cost, of goodwill in the Western business community. If the apparent benefits to the USSR of that goodwill are lost, such a re-examination would have serious repercussions in Eastern and Western Europe.

One result would be that the more conservative factions in the Kremlin would be strengthened, the economies would become more, not less, centralised and the East European economies more integrated into the Soviet bloc. Alternatively, the maintenance of East–West trade could bring increased pressure for domestic reforms to encourage the Soviet Union and Eastern Europe to market their products in the West. Inevitably the most likely outcome is a compromise, in which certain East European countries continue on the path to economic reform, while the USSR maintains a broadly centralised economy, utilising its exports of energy sources and raw materials to earn enough hard currency to cover desired purchases from the West.

5 Agriculture
Alec Nove

The subject of agriculture is infinitely fascinating and changing. Many years ago when Radio Erevan was still functioning, a listener asked: 'Can there by a way out of a totally hopeless situation?' Radio Erevan replied: 'We do not discusss agriculture on this programme'. There is a tendency in the Soviet Union to regard agriculture as a fairly hopeless sector. Even Brezhnev was prepared to admit that the problem of feeding the population is extremely urgent, more urgent than problems of energy and transport. Bearing in mind the problems facing energy and transport, it is clear that the Soviet leadership regards agriculture, its recovery and advance, as a matter of the highest priority. In this respect, it must be emphasised that the picture has altogether changed compared with, say, the days of Stalin. At that time agriculture was regarded as a resource to be exploited for the benefit of the rest of the economy. This meant poorly-paid peasants and low investment. In those days if one discussed the reasons for the poor performance of agriculture, one spoke in such terms. It was neglected, it was under-capitalised and there were few labour incentives, so naturally productivity was low. What one is now dealing with, however, is a completely different situation. Far from being exploited for the benefit of the rest of the economy, agriculture has become a millstone or ball and chain around the rest of the economy. Agriculture now takes 27 per cent of total Soviet investment, which is a very high figure by any international standard. The state budget pays out, in annual subsidies to cover the losses of the *kolkhoz* (collective) and state farm sector, a sum which looks like being 27 to 28 billion roubles in 1982. This is substantially more than the Soviet Union admits to spending on defence, and is by far the largest agricultural subsidy in human history. Far from deriving revenues from agriculture, they are diverting revenues from other sectors of the economy to agriculture.

Any analysis of Soviet agriculture, therefore, must focus on the reasons for the poor performance of a high priority sector. The question that must be asked is why, despite the, surely, sincere endeavours of the leadership to put matters right, and their willingness to pay very large sums to do so, the situation remains so bad that food shortages are endemic, despite large imports, especially of grain, but also of meat and butter, from the West. There seem to be two factors, not themselves connected with the Soviet agricultural system, that must be mentioned.

One is the weather. It is not the fault of the leadership that the Soviet Union is in a climatic zone, adversely affected by drought, winter kill and other natural disasters. The very considerable variation in the Soviet harvest is clearly due to these climatic handicaps. Anyone wishing to compare the performances of American and Soviet agriculture, would have to put quite high on the list of different factors the United States' more reliable rainfall, longer periods of sunshine and, generally speaking, more fertile soil and fewer climatic handicaps. To make matters worse, the Soviet Union has now experienced three bad weather years in a row, which is rather exceptional. The difference between the record harvest of almost 240 million tonnes in 1978 and the 1981 harvest of perhaps 170 million tonnes, is obviously due, not to changes of policy, nor to the Soviet system, but to much less favourable weather.

The second factor is price policy. One does not need to be a professional economist to know that shortages are related to prices. The last increase in the price of basic foodstuffs occurred in the Soviet Union 20 years ago. Since then aggregate money income of the population has doubled. Not very surprisingly for people who for very many years lived on a diet of potatoes, cabbage and bread, the extra money has turned itself into a very sharply increased demand for livestock products in general and meat in particular. Therefore, as was also the case in Poland, part of the reason for the shortages is the obstinate refusal of the authorities to raise prices to an economically reasonable level. Similarly, the cheapest bread in the Soviet Union at the moment is by far the cheapest cattle and pig feed and this could cause a shortage of even ordinary bread. This has not yet happened, but peasants do go to town, buy as much cheap bread as possible to feed their animals because it is extremely cheap and there is very little other fodder to buy. Thus part of the problem concerns prices, and the authorities' reluctance to raise them. However when the Polish leadership tried to raise prices they ran into riots and civil commotion, and maybe the Soviet leaders too are afraid of this. Be that as it may, one must not leave prices out of any analysis of shortages and of the causes of the present difficulties that face the ordinary citizen.

However everyone in the Soviet Union from Andropov down would agree that neither climate nor prices offer a satisfactory explanation. There is a malfunctioning of the system. Despite all the handicaps and all the difficulties, they ought to be producing more. It is now necessary to examine, point by point those factors which are holding back Soviet agricultural production and which make the very large investments that have been made relatively ineffective, and then to discuss what they propose to do about this and whether these proposals will help.

There is no dispute about the list of negative factors which follow. There can, of course, be arguments about how relatively important each factor is, but all of them are repeatedly found in the Soviet press. Therefore the list is not controversial.

Let us begin with one that a number of Soviet economists regard as crucial. This is the problem of labour: peasants, incentives and the willingness to work. Fedor Abramov, a well known writer of peasant origin, recently wrote in *Pravda* about revisiting his native village:

When was it known that ablebodied peasants would leave the village at the time of the harvest rush? The old pride in a well ploughed field, in a well sown crop, in well looked after livestock, is disappearing. Is not this the cause of absenteeism, of lateness, of drunkenness? . . . There is the fear of upsetting one's fellow villagers. All hope for a strict and fair *nachalnik* [boss], who will arrive from somewhere and impose order. Almost like the poet Nekrasov: 'The master will come and judge us' [*Vot priyedet barin, barin nas rassudit*].

This kind of plea, a genuine cry from the heart, finds its echo in other published contributions in *Pravda* and elsewhere. More than ten years ago Soviet agricultural officials were making this point about peasant commitment, or rather the lack of commitment to work, being a major issue. One official said that the peasant attitude can be summed up thus: 'We will sow, God will send rain and people will come from the town to bring in the harvest'. He pointed out that in all countries peasants on farms, when the harvest rush is on, work from dawn to dusk, except in the Soviet Union, where they work a seven-hour day and then go home; or even to market to sell cabbages or flowers. There is no sense of responsibility. As a result of this, he said, and as a result also of inadequate mechanisation, it is necessary to import many millions of people from the towns to cope with the harvest peak demand for labour.

According to E. Manevich (*Voprosy Ekonomiki* 9/1981), a labour economist, in an article on the use and misuse of labour in the Soviet Union, the total number of people who are annually mobilised to cope with the harvest, amounts to 15.6 million. It seems an incredibly high figure! He went on to say that if they spend one day getting to the village and one day getting back, that represents a loss to the rest of the economy of 31.2 million worker days. Their productivity is much lower than that of the regular labour force and much lower than it would have been in their own factories. He adds that about eight million of them come from the productive sectors of the economy. The rest include millions of students, a large part of the Soviet army and all kinds of other odds and ends.

Absenteeism, indifference and unwillingness to make an effort are reinforced by a further feature of the system, the failure to link incentives to the final result of the work done. The classic example, and it has been quoted repeatedly, is the tractor driver who is paid for ploughing and is on piece-rates; that is to say, he is paid according to the number of hectares he ploughs. He also collects a bonus for saving fuel and for minimising breakages. He can achieve all three objectives by ploughing as shallow as possible, and the fact that he is paid well for this compounds the problem. That shallow ploughing may have an unfortunate effect on the harvest is not his business, and of course the size of the harvest may be due to other causes too. Consequently, the effect of incentives is sometimes negative. Both the negative attitude of the peasants and the way the incentives work in practice, can be seen as a kind of diseconomy of scale. The farms are too big for peasants to be interested in the outcome of their work, too big for effective management, too big for the proper organisation of work.

In 1955, one British farmer with a British agricultural delegation, observing a collective farm, said a farm as big and complex as that could only be managed by a genius. 'Are you sure', he asked the Soviet officials, 'that you have enough geniuses?' There is a lot of truth in this. Unless people are willing to work, and in agriculture it is difficult to supervise workers effectively, since they are scattered over a wide area, other, doubtless much needed, measures will have only limited effect.

The Soviet economist Fedorova (*Voprosy ekonomiki* 12/1975: 57) has pointed out that in agriculture almost all women's work is unskilled and dull. Mechanised work is overwhelmingly male, as is supervising (except in dairy farming which is predominantly female). 'Why is this so?', she asks. One of the reasons given, apart from tradition, is that, for example, tractors are so badly designed and so difficult to operate that it has become an extremely heavy job and as such is considered unsuitable for women, so that only 0.5 per cent of all tractor and combine harvester drivers in the Soviet Union are women.

Previously the level of education in the village was low; now everyone is educated to the age of 16. So there are girls who have gone through secondary school and find that there is absolutely no skilled work for them to do in the village. They want to get out, and become discontented and disillusioned. Many of them do go to town in the end, despite all the limitations on movement, and young men begin to leave the village because of the lack of girls. This is the reverse of the situation after the war, when as a result of war losses girls were trying to leave the villages because there were not enough men.

There appears to be general agreement that the situation has got gradually worse. According to the article by Manevich the 15.6 million people now being mobilised to bring in the harvest represented a 2.4-fold increase over 1970. Yet mechanisation should have reduced the labour shortage.

One reason why peasants are unwilling to work is that they become dispirited at being ordered to do work which they know to be nonsense. They may be aware, for example, that one should not sow in the mud, but a party secretary might order this to be done so that he could report to Moscow that the sowing in his region has been completed by the date prescribed in the plan.

This is an example of another source of inefficiency, excessive interference from above. Managers of these large farms, their agronomists and technical specialists have decisions imposed on them. This, again, is an old standing complaint. We have it on the authority of Brezhnev's own memoirs: excessive tutelage and control of farms from above is a major source of weakness. Then why can't party officials stop these practices? There are at least two decrees on the need to stop them. The first was in 1955, in the days of Khrushchev, and the other was in 1982. According to *Pravda*:

Too many compulsory indicators are imposed from above . . . particularly frequent is the prescription of areas to be sown. An agronomist, in practice, cannot decide for himself what to sow, exact figures are imposed on him, and he is always compelled to carry out these orders. Thus some farms have been forbidden to reduce the area under potatoes . . . Although the party has always condemned the practice of giving detailed orders this style has not disappeared . . . Thus the oblast agricultural department calls in our specialist and orders him to double the area sown to maize this spring, but where can he find the area without ruining our crop rotation? (26 March 1982).

Why regulate our everyday activities; what field to sow on Friday and which on Saturday, where to have clean fallow and where not. Surely this is a matter for the competent specialists. Yet until now the party secretary has told us where and when to plough. (11 May 1982)

Why *do* they go on doing it? According to party decisions, the only compulsory indicators ought to be those connected with the compulsory deliveries of crops and livestock products to the state. The rest ought to be within the competence of the collective and state farms to decide. But this, in fact, does not happen. Is it traditional distrust of the peasant which lies deep in the official mind?

Other sectors of the economy are planned, but not in such detail. If the manager of a factory is ordered to produce a certain quantity of ball bearings or coal or skirts, he is allowed to get on with it and is not told how to do it in detail. But farm managers are. Despite having adopted decrees which state that the farms should not be subject to detailed plans, the same centre that issues these decrees proceeds to produce a whole string of new decrees. For example, in May 1982, a decree was published imposing upon the ministry, the local party and agricultural officials the duty to ensure that farms carry out a variety of instructions, thus guaranteeing that the very interference which has been condemned on the one hand will be insisted upon on the other. The farms are too big anyway and the imposition of orders on farms from above is certainly another, and well recognised, cause of loss and inefficiency which breeds, as managements admit, a sense of irresponsibility. After all, in the last resort, they are not responsible. Since they are ordered about, they become apathetic and regard themselves as a cog in a vast machine, instead of using their initiative to adapt what is happening on the farm to the very varied circumstances that arise in farming.

It is necessary now to turn to the question of equipment and mechanisation. During his time in office, Brezhnev repeatedly spoke about this, and decrees on the subject of agricultural machinery constantly refer to the poor quality of the machines and appallingly low levels of repair and maintenance. The last of these have several causes. One is the lack of qualified people in the village to do this type of work. Second is the lack of spare parts, which are supposedly supplied but never seem to arrive. Third is the lack of necessary equipment or sometimes of any sort of workshop. Fourth is often an incredible lack of the most elementary shelter or cover. Machines, for instance, are left out in the rain and snow. Many cartoons in the satirical journal *Krokodil* illustrate this. In one, a visitor asks: 'Why do you leave all this valuable machinery outside without any cover?' 'What do you mean', replies the manager, 'it's covered in snow, isn't it?'

The failure to deliver the needed machines and spare parts is a consequence of the deficiencies of industrial planning. One of the basic problems of the entire economic system is the weak position of the customer *vis-à-vis* the supplier. The customer has insufficient influence over what is produced. Brezhnev himself stated this, so it is not in dispute. Farms frequently cannot obtain the machines they require. The agricultural machinery industry is overloaded with orders it cannot fulfil. It has aggregate plans of machinery, expressed in tonnes and/or roubles. Faced with excess planned demand, it naturally produces those things which will add up most easily to the right aggregate plan figures. However this results in *nekompleksnost*, as it is called in Russian, about which an enormous amount is written in the Soviet press. For effective mechanisation, one needs a series of machines which will carry out, in an efficient manner, consecutive agricultural processes. For example, one may have a combine harvester which harvests a lot of grain which piles up, but there is no loading and unloading machinery and a lack of storage space. The lack of *kompleksnaya mekhanizatsiya* is illustrated by the fate of the Soviet equivalent of the Massey-Harris-Ferguson type of tractor, which can be used with a very large number of labour-saving attachments. The factories produce this very effective tractor, but instead of producing 30 needed attachments, they only provide five.

Another example concerns fodder for livestock, which is in short supply. There are big machines for cutting hay, but in the Soviet Union as elsewhere quite a lot of grass grows in inconvenient places for large machines; on verges of roads, in woods, railway embankments, for example. They need a small grass cutter to do this work. It is also needed urgently, for private livestock owners to cut grass for their own animals. A decision was taken many years ago to produce them, but they are still not available. *Pravda* sent a correspondent to ask a factory manager why. 'After all,' said the correspondent, 'they are simple and cheap'. The answer he received was: it is because they are simple and cheap that they are not being produced because they do not count much towards plan fulfilment in the agricultural machinery industry.

Furthermore a state organisation, *Selkhoztekhnika*, stands between the agricultural machinery industry and the farms. It is also its task to provide spare parts and repair facilities. It has been criticised very sharply indeed, and repeatedly, for not doing what needs to be done, and it even systematically cheats the farms. *Pravda* alone printed four articles in 1982 saying that farms repeatedly find that if they ask for spare parts for repairs in their own workshops, *Selkhoztekhnika* provides them on condition that the farms sign a document stating that the repairs have been done in *Selkhoztekhnika*'s workshops, and make them pay for these mythical repairs. Another farm reported that it needed certain machines and was told to go and collect them. So it sent a lorry about 300 kilometres to the factory to collect the machines which were supplied in pieces for it to assemble. It took the machines back to its own ill-equipped workshop and tried to assemble them. It then received a bill from *Selkhoztekhnika* for transport, testing and assembly. What was *Selkhoztekhnika*'s defence? Simply that it has a plan to fulfil in roubles.

There are a large number of articles under the heading *Selo i ego partnery* (the village and its partners) which point out that what is needed in the end is the harvest and not the fulfilment of plans in roubles by service agencies.

Another classic example of planning errors relates to mineral fertiliser. While its output has gone up, it is not being very effectively used since there is a shortage of bags to put it in, shelters to keep it in, transport to get it to the farms and machinery to spread it over the fields. Long ago Khrushchev remarked that there were pile-ups of fertiliser at railheads which, awaiting transport in winter, became covered in snow, much to the convenience of children going sledging. More examples can be borrowed from *Krokodil*. Cartoon one: railway and mountains, with a goat on top of one of the peaks. A passenger says to the guard. 'Mountains? Are we already in the Caucasus?' 'No, no', says the guard, 'that is potash, over there are nitrogenous fertilisers, we'll get to the Caucasus tomorrow.' Second cartoon: again a railway, again piles of fertiliser along the railway line, as a result of which the telegraph poles have begun to sprout. Third cartoon: again a pile of fertiliser, this time in a village. It is pouring with rain and it is out in the open. A visitor says to the farm chairman. 'This is outrageous, what will an inspector say?' And the farm chairman replies. 'What inspector would get here on these roads?'

The serious side of this subject is infrastructure; first and foremost, roads or rather the lack of them. Anyone who knows the Soviet Union well will be aware that the great Russian plain turns into deep mud when it rains. Russian roads, after being traversed in mud, dry out and leave deep ruts. Driving along these roads is quite an experience. A chairman of a *kolkhoz* in Kursk oblast wrote to *Pravda* to say that his farm is only six kilometres from a main highway, but that for many months of the year only caterpillar tractors can drag his lorries to that road and that this state of affairs is an absolute disaster.

A number of eminent Soviet specialists on transport know conditions are poor and publish articles on the cost of not having an adequate road network. It is no accident that one area of the Soviet Union where agriculture does quite well, Estonia, also happens to be an area with a good road network inherited from the days of independence.

A report on the subject in *Novy Mir* gave one example of the failure of massive investments: the building of a very sophisticated and extremely modern piggery but with no access road, so for much of the year it is not possible to reach it. This illustrates *nekompleksnost*, not this time of machinery but of investment planning. One may well ask why this lack of co-ordination occurs, given the fact that the Soviet Union has a planned economy. The answer is quite straightforward: while at the top it *should* be co-ordinated, at the operational level it is divided among many different departments, and they draft their own orders. The department responsible for fertiliser production is not responsible for the machinery that spreads it or for the bags to put it in, because that is the responsibility of other departments. Railway bottlenecks, of course, are the responsibility of the Ministry of Transport. Road building involves a different ministry, and so on. Co-ordination is the task of planners at the centre but they are very heavily overloaded and the task is simply beyond them.

Let us now turn to the problem of the private plot. It has, of course, been a valuable source of food and revenue for the peasant for a long time. It is still, according to the figures that have been published. It provides most of the food of villagers, other than bread, though not quite to the same extent as formerly. Similarly it provides the peasant with a fairly considerable amount of money from the sale of produce, although no longer the major part, as it used to be when the peasant received hardly any remuneration for work on the collective farm. Peasants are now very much better paid for collective and state farm-work. Nevertheless, the private plot is important and it is growing in significance in the consciousness of the leadership as one way of resolving the short and medium-term food problem. Figures published in late 1981 reveal that the output of the private plot accounts for 26 per cent of agricultural output, and this despite some obstruction on the part of the authorities. It has been reported that peasants are not provided with transport to get their produce to town; there are no packaging materials; it is difficult to sell through state and co-operative agencies, although provision for this exists; the agencies lack incentive to handle perishables, and themselves lack transport and storage facilities. Then there are difficulties over pasture rights, obtaining fodder for private livestock and so on. Livestock is very important, since according to the same statistics close to two-thirds of the value of private production consists of livestock products.

This is one reason for criticising those who assert that although private plots only cover 3 per cent of the arable land, they provide approximately 26 per cent of the output, implying that they are over eight times more efficient than collective or state farms. This is an improper comparison: two-thirds of the output is livestock products, and private animals are not fed on the private plots but on pasture outside them. In any case if one only has a very limited amount of land, one naturally puts high value crops on it. In Georgia, for example, one plants lemons, in Russia proper it would be vegetables and fruit. Naturally the value of the output per hectare will be higher than the same area under wheat or rye. Nonetheless, it is true that yields on private plots do tend to be higher. They are a very important source of food supply and certainly the discouragement of private plot production has contributed to shortages in the large towns.

Soviet policy towards the private plot has zigzagged over the years. First the leadership wanted full collectivisation; they thought they could do without it. They found that they could not. Stalin made a joke to the effect that there had been a 'misunderstanding with peasant women on the subject of cows'. (This was Stalin's way of changing his mind without making a formal policy statement.) Later, still under Stalin, they imposed heavy taxes and high delivery obligations on the private plot. In 1953 Khrushchev denounced this policy, and taxes were reduced, delivery obligations ceased and the private plot was encouraged. But restrictions were again being imposed at the end of the Khrushchev era, and when Brezhnev became party leader in 1964, he criticised Khrushchev for his negative attitude towards the private plot. However under Brezhnev too, private production was again held back by various obstacles.

These took some extraordinary forms. *Pravda* reported that one unfortunate man succeeded in getting the loan of a small van from his *kolkhoz*. He loaded it with vegetables and was making his way to the nearest town, Rostov-on-Don, when a policeman stopped him. He was informed that he would only be allowed to go to Rostov-on-Don if he delivered his vegetables to state procurement agencies; on the way back his weighbill and receipt would be checked. (All this was quite illegal.) He went to Rostov-on-Don and found that owing to the lack of storage space no one wanted his produce. And yet he was going to get into trouble with the police on the way home. A Catch-22 situation. Similar examples were cited in a recent *Pravda* article entitled 'The Worker' (23 August 1982).

The Soviet leadership is quite sincere about the fact that the food shortage calls for drastic measures, but in deciding what to do it suffers from built-in limitations. An article by the Hungarian émigré, George Markus, discussed this very point. He asked: do the regimes in Eastern Europe want to increase agricultural production as fast as possible? Yes. What then is the cheapest and quickest way of ensuring an increase in agricultural production? Encourage the private plot. What is the second cheapest? Co-operatives and collective farms. What is the dearest and the least efficient? State farms. What they invariably do is to put most of their money into state farms, less money into collective farms and obstruct the private plot (*Praxis international no.* 3, 1981). He says that the reason for this apparent contradiction is that one of their primary objectives is to maximise the degree to which the state, the party and the planning apparatus control the product. From this point of view, state farms come first, collective farms second and the private plot last, so they face a contradiction.

Michael Ellman has also pointed out that there is in the Marxist tradition a gross overestimation of the economies of scale in agriculture, and a gross underestimation of the diseconomies of large-scale agriculture. It goes against established habits to divide up the gigantic farms. In fact, for years they have been increasing their size through amalgamation. What are they now to do? One suggestion is to establish agro-industrial complexes. In itself this is not a bad idea in certain spheres. For example, there is no reason why, if one is growing tomatoes, there should not be a cannery, which might also give employment to people at slack periods of the year. Nor is there any reason why there should not be quite a large number of factory farms for the production of chickens, eggs and so on in the Soviet Union. Within reason, and if the necessary resources are available, this is excellent. Unfortunately it looks like developing into a party-led campaign. Its latest manifestation is the decree issued in May 1982, which involves co-ordination of the work of farms and their so called 'partners'. Processing, the production of the packaging materials, supply of machinery, repairs, the spreading of fertiliser and pesticides and transport ought to be put under one organisational umbrella to ensure that they are all locally co-ordinated, according to this decree. In itself the idea seems to be quite a good one but it looks like becoming a complex bureaucratic structure which will certainly conflict with the notion of letting farm managers adjust to the circumstances they face on the spot.

In Hungary, where agriculture is much more successful, there are agro-industrial complexes but on a strictly voluntary basis. Any Hungarian co-operative which wishes to join others in such a complex is free to do so and is free not to do so, if it so desires, or to walk out. It is unlikely, however, that the voluntary principle would be adhered to in the Soviet Union and the result would inevitably be a bureaucratic mess. In this connection it is worth quoting a very wise statement by a former Soviet state farm director. Khrushchev had just abolished the Machine Tractor Stations (MTS) which had serviced the collective farms. When asked whether it was a good idea, he replied that it was a serious error. Before the abolition of the MTS, collective farms had been forbidden to buy tractors and combine harvesters. After the abolition they were forbidden *not* to buy tractors and combine harvesters. The correct solution all along would have been to allow those which wanted to buy them, to do so and to allow those which wanted to hire them, to hire them; bearing in mind that some have workshops and others have not, some have skilled labour while others have none.

Much can be learned from this. What is needed is much greater variety, flexibility and spontaneity.

There are other, more positive, policies being adopted. Firstly, there is what looks like a genuinely new policy towards the private plot. Whether this will last longer than previous policies is not yet clear, but much publicity has been given to the need to encourage in particular the raising of private livestock. This policy includes granting the family additional land on which to grow fodder crops or raise their own livestock and contracts for the delivery of the necessary fodder, on condition the meat is sold to the state, at favourable prices. (State meat is now quite expensive, as are potatoes.) There is some relaxation of the strict limits on the number of livestock which can be kept by peasants, and there is willingness to learn in all these respects from the successful Hungarian experiment, where a very lively private livestock sector contributes to the quantities of food – as everyone who goes to Budapest can see – in the markets and the shops. It is worth noting that in Hungary it is beginning to be difficult to distinguish between what is private and what is collective, since some of the pigs that are fattened by private households may, in fact, be technically collective farm pigs. They are looked after on contract by the private household and are sold to the state food industry either directly or through the farms. This merging, in an attractive and remunerative way, of private, co-operative and state enterprise has operated quite efficiently in Hungary, and may do so in the USSR as well. This would represent genuine progress so we must watch and see how it develops in practice.

Then there is the problem of the *beznaryadnoe zveno* or autonomous work team. *Naryad* is a work assignment, *beznaryadnoe* is 'without a work assignment'. The *zveno* or link (usually about seven persons) has been used since time immemorial but labour in general is normally given detailed assignments. The idea of the autonomous work team has been discussed off and on for over 15 years. It consists of taking a group of about seven peasants, putting them in charge of the cultivation of some crop or crops on an area of land, perhaps for several years, plus the necessary equipment. They are left to organise their own work and are paid by results. If this group has a tractor, it is no longer necessary for an inspector to walk around to ensure that the driver ploughs deep. Why should he plough shallow? He is part of the same small work group whose pay depends on the harvest. There is a direct link between effort and cost, and between effort and result.

Articles favouring this kind of *zveno* appeared in *Pravda*, for example, on 5 November 1979, 14 July 1980, 26 March 1981 and 25 May 1981. All these articles stated that experiments on these lines had been successfully carried out and one asked rather naively why this experiment had not been extended and why this could not be done on a national scale? However, the original proposal dates back to the late 1960s. At the Agricultural Economists' Conference in Minsk in 1970, the then Minister of Agriculture, V.V. Matskevich, was asked whether he thought it was a good idea. His reply was remarkably brief: 'No'.

Why not? One might think that the main reason is that it breaks up the farm into small units, and small units could give too direct a family interest in the land, which would be ideologically unacceptable. There may be something in this. But there are other reasons of a more practical kind. One of these is that by no means all jobs on the farm can be organised in this way. Some activities are very seasonal. Some crops cannot be looked after by such small groups. I was told privately that the adoption of such a system creates tension on the farm, since payment by results makes for very large income differentials. In particular women field workers, the unskilled general labourers, are not put into these little groups because skilled people are needed who can operate machines and work hard. So women will lose out. They not only might but do complain.

The Soviet Union is an odd place in this respect. Of course, there are privileges and there is inequality but there is also an egalitarian ethos. The planning system – also in industry – has tended to equalise conditions for groups of workers. This can be illustrated by looking at the reasons why the famous 'Shchekino experiment' did not work out. This was a method which intended to encourage higher productivity by allowing the factories to keep the wages which they saved through shedding surplus labour. One reason was that the authorities were reluctant to allow surplus labour to be dismissed, but the other is that the entire scheme conflicts with the principle of equal pay for equal work or effort. It was argued that a factory might be able to shed labour because it had a large labour surplus, while its neighbours were more honest and did not hoard labour, and that as a result of their honesty they would earn less than the other factory. This is regarded as unfair, and strong pressures arise to combat 'undeserved' pay increases.

Similarly, the communist party has adopted an ambiguous attitude to the *beznaryadnoe zveno*. At one point it allowed discussion, then it suppressed it, and one of the chief supporters of the scheme in distant Kazakhstan was even arrested – though not for proposing the *beznaryadnoe zveno*, they got him on some other pretext. For nearly ten years discussion lapsed but now it has revived. Although *Pravda* and other journals publish discussions and articles, usually by chairmen of *kolkhozes* or by agronomists, there has not been any party pronouncement on it. Preference has been given to the *brigadnyi podryad*, or contract work by field and livestock brigades, which may represent a sort of compromise.

Apart from experimenting with the *baznaryadnoe zveno*, the Soviet Union ought to break up its gigantic farms into smaller units which have some kind of coherence and are more manageable. Here there is a lot the Soviets can learn from the Hungarians. The relative success of Hungarian co-operative farms is, to a considerable extent, due to two factors which are noticeably absent from the Soviet scene. The Hungarian farms, for most of the time, are free to decide what to grow, what to sell, how to operate, how to organise their work, and so on. The absence of systematic and continuous interference and the absence of compulsory deliveries create an important advantage for the Hungarians. This is not to say that there is no state interference; there can be a telephone call telling the farm to grow more barley, but this is exceptional and not systematic. Secondly, Hungarian farms, as a result of the adoption of the economic reform in industry, are able to purchase their own inputs without administrative allocation.

The clumsy Soviet allocation system is a by product of centralised industrial planning, and the problem is exacerbated by the fact that the farms as customers, like all other customers, are in such a weak position. They cannot simply buy, they have to write and beg for a material allocation, as everything is administratively distributed. In Hungary, it is all much simpler, and supplies can be bought in state stores; even a mini-cement mixer for private building is obtainable, as well as building materials, spades, hoes and small tools, all of which are extremely scarce in the Soviet Union. Hence the Soviets have a lot to learn from the Hungarians.

However, abandoning the compulsory allocation of materials would be contrary to established habits and traditions. To enable the farms freely to purchase all they need, without going through the elaborate allocation system, requires major reform, not in agriculture but in industry. A major economic reform is required which the present Soviet leadership appears unwilling to contemplate. They are prepared to go on spending enormous sums trying to solve their agricultural problems. However, progress will be slow and Soviet agriculture will remain a burden on the rest of the economy, although it must be stated that it is much more productive than it was 20 or 30 years ago.

Turning now to the complex problem of relations with the United States, experience has taught the Soviets that they should aim at a higher degree of self-sufficiency, and indeed the decisions of May 1982 specifically state this. They seem to be aiming at a level of grain production which would only necessitate imports in an outstandingly bad year; they would have an export surplus, as they used to have in days gone by, in extremely good years. That would seem a normal and reasonable aim. They also speak of the necessity of building up reserves, and have a very big programme building grain elevators and the like. Of course, the risk of embargoes worries them. One recalls Frederick Forsyth's novel *The Devil's Alternative* in which the Politburo, faced with a disastrous harvest, contemplated a Third World War as a possible solution. But of course that was fiction!

Americans achieve their present diet on the basis of one tonne of grain per head of the population. For the Soviet Union, this means, roughly 270 million tonnes. They say that their long-term aim is to achieve a grain harvest of this magnitude, in order to sustain a pattern of consumption of livestock products and the number of livestock in the American model. This is a consequence of the persistence of low prices for livestock products. If they took their courage in both hands and sharply increased the price of these products, they could reduce their subsidy bill and make it possible for them to cover their domestic requirements at a lower level. But if they achieve, let us say, an average harvest of 220 million tonnes, it will still be insufficient, at present prices, to supply enough meat and livestock products, because Soviet animals eat relatively more grain than American livestock, due to the lack of other fodder.

In a number of Soviet analyses the question is posed: why are we feeding grain concentrates in such awesome quantities? The answer is that root crops have low yields, there is not enough hay and so on. The livestock diet is unbalanced, there is not enough protein, and they discuss using more fish meal and synthetic proteins of various kinds in order to relieve the pressure on grain. While the aim is to achieve self-sufficiency in normal years, they are unlikely to achieve this even if they do put up the price of meat. If they do not, there is not the slightest chance of their achieving their target.

Some Western economists have suggested that there is no need for the Soviet Union to achieve self-sufficiency in grain or livestock products. Any shortfalls could be bought on the international market. American farmers, especially, are very keen to sell to the Soviet Union.

There are two basic reasons why reliance on the international market would be inadvisable. One is that the quantities needed are so large that the world market could not supply them. It is a fair assumption that the Soviet consumption of meat is about 15 million tonnes and that the grain harvest in 1981, which was a bad year, was about 170 million tonnes. These figures represent considerably more than the total international trade in the commodities concerned. Consequently, a large part has to be produced domestically. True, if additional domestic production is very expensive, some reliance on imports has its attractions. In a world which is settled and peaceful, this would make sense, but it renders them vulnerable in the event of international tension.

The second reason why they do not wish to rely on imports in the long term is that they believe, and not without reason, that, whereas agriculture is costly and inefficient now, it could become much more efficient in the future. The whole object of their present endeavours is to achieve that level of efficiency. Unfortunately, while production has risen in the last 20–30 years, if one measures efficiency in terms of the cost of production, it has ballooned upwards, because of one-sided, unbalanced mechanisation and higher labour costs. The machines are expensive, they have many defects and agriculture has become more complicated because of mechanisation. The supply system, which was never good, has to respond to ever more complex challenges, and does so badly. As a result, costs have mounted rapidly, which is one reason for the enormous increase in the food subsidy.

It is interesting to compare relative costs of agricultural production in the Soviet Union and in other countries. It cannot be done directly through an official rate of exchange. What can be done is to compare costs with the cost of other things in roubles, and by any standard the cost of Soviet agriculture is high. This is also true of Common Market agriculture, compared with the USA and Canada, but even in comparison with Western Europe, Soviet costs are high. Some parts of the Soviet economy, the defence sector for example, are efficient. So how does one explain the limited success achieved in agriculture, given that the resources and the desire to succeed are great?

In assessing relative efficiency, it is useful to stress two aspects:

priority and planability. When the two come together – easy to plan and high priority – the system works quite well. A pertinent example is electricity generation which is centralised in most countries, including Britain; the product is homogenous, planable and regarded as very important. Here the Soviets have a good record. There is nothing in the system which should prevent the energy sector being well planned. However a situation can arise where there is a high degree of priority and a low ability to plan. I think agriculture is one example, but another is technical progress.

Agriculture and the diffusion of modern technology are two very different things – but they have one thing in common, that the centre cannot and does not know the microeconomic detail. The centre can assign agriculture priority, but some stupid official in, say, Tambov oblast, will order a farm to sow a field to barley, though this might conflict with local conditions, and the labour and machinery necessary may not be available. The unfortunate farm will then apply for the necessary machinery to cultivate the barley but a remote official may refuse it. The centre does not and cannot concern itself with such detail. It is in the same position *vis-à-vis* technical progress. The Poliburo does not know which kind of device should be applied or precisely which machine a given factory should be producing. So a situation arises in which there is high priority and low planability. Even if a large amount of money is invested, the result is disappointing.

In an article in *Pravda* in May 1982, it was pointed out that in the field of armaments there is competition. 'We have to compare our product all the time with those produced abroad', and 'what a pity this is not done in the case of civilian machinery.' There is competition between design bureaux. There are a number of famous aircraft designers, Tupolev and Yakovlev for example, who have built up their own design bureaux and these, in effect, compete with one another. So a combination of all these factors allied to the fact that military orders are given priority through the bureaucratic maze, ensures that they actually do get what they need. In the case of armaments the state itself is the customer. State farms, although owned by the state, have just not got the same authority. In this respect a gun or tank is in quite a different category to a harrow or potato digger.

New measures
In May 1982, the plenary session of the Central Committee of the Communist Party of the Soviet Union adopted a 'food programme for the USSR for the period up to 1990'. This document and the related decrees are a reflection of the deep concern which the food shortages are causing the leadership, and represent its ideas as to which are the most urgent measures to set things right.

The essential features of these measures are as follows:

(i) *Organisational*. As already indicated, the numerous organisations involved in the whole complex of agriculture, and the processing, packing and transporting of produce to the consumers, are often at cross-purposes, serving different masters. A new hierarchy of co-ordinators, with powers over these various organisations, is being created, with a deputy Prime Minister in charge of it at the centre. Such organs will exist also in republics, oblasts and localities. (One wonders whether this will not introduce still more complexities into the already complicated structure of ministerial and party control).

(ii) *Financial, investment and price policies*. Another substantial increase has been announced in prices paid to farms, an increase which will be worth the very large annual sum of 16 billion roubles, with effect from January 1983. Many farms' debts to the State Bank will be written off. Much more will be spent on infrastructure, packaging materials, storage space, rural roads and village amenities. The 'agro-industrial complex' will absorb 33 per cent of total investments.

(iii) *Labour incentives* will be more directly related to final results, i.e. the size of the harvest and livestock production, with more use of small groups of labourers paid in relation to the output they produce. A larger proportion of pay will be in kind, reversing the tendency to pay *kolkhoz* members and state farm workers predominantly in cash.

(iv) Efforts will be made to improve the quality, range and reliability of *machinery* and deliveries of *fertiliser* (at present close to 20 per cent of all fertiliser is said to be lost in transport, and the chemical content is frequently unsuitable for the soil to which it is applied).

(v) The programme announces *targets* for 1990. These are given in Table 5.1, which contrasts them with the performance of recent years.

Table 5.1   Agricultural production: some physical data (million tonnes, annual averages

	1966–70 average	1965–71 average	1976–80 average	1981	1981–5[a] plan	1985–90 plan
Grain	167.6	181.6	205.0	(170)[b]	238–43	250–5
Vegetables	19.7	23.0	26.3	25.6	n.a.	37–9
Meat	11.6	14.0	14.8	15.2	17–17.5	20–20.;
Milk	80.6	87.4	92.7	88.5	97–9	104–06
Eggs (billion)	35.8	51.4	63.1	67.9	72	78–9
Potatoes	94.8	89.8	82.6	72.0	—	—
Sugar beet	81.1	76.0	88.4	60.5	—	—

[a] These targets may be intended to relate to the last years of the quinquennium.
[b] No official figure for the grain harvest for 1981 has yet been published.
Source of plan figures Brezhnev, *Pravda* 25 May 1982.

The figures show that output did indeed rise in the period after 1965, but incomes rose much faster, with prices frozen, and since 1975 growth came to a halt. ('Meat consumption per capita did not increase, milk and fruit consumption even fell' *Voprosy ekonomiki* no. 7, 1982: 6). The targets set seem decidedly optimistic. There should be some limited improvement, but surely not to the envisaged levels.

6 Foreign Trade Policy: The USSR, The West and Eastern Europe as an Eternal Triangle
Philip Hanson

Introduction

The makers of Soviet foreign trade policy seem in the last decade to have been oscillating between two magnetic poles, whose powers both to attract and repel have constantly fluctuated. On the one hand there is the allure, even in recession, of Western plenty and dealing with the West offers large potential economic gains, but at a political risk. On the other hand there is the burden of Empire in Eastern Europe*: here the potential unity of the Soviet bloc must be maintained, at a considerable economic cost to Moscow. To complicate the Soviet policy-makers' choices (and to overstretch an already well-stretched metaphor), these two magnetic poles both attract and repel one another.

The nature of the restless triangular relationship is the subject of the present chapter. It will be argued that Soviet policy choices in foreign trade in the 1980s are likely to continue to entail an awkward series of compromises between the two spheres of activity.

It should be remembered throughout that these are the trade policy decisions of a country whose trade is less important to it than most countries. The exact share of trade in the economy is not something that can be easily measured. (The arithmetic means of merchandise imports and exports, as a percentage of Gross National Product (GNP), is a conventional measure.) The fact that domestic transactions are carried out in prices that bear no systematic relationship to the prices of foreign transactions makes such estimates problematic. For the late 1970s it is possible to come up with percentages that range from 4 to 12. The lowest figure is the outcome of dividing official Soviet trade data (converted into dollars at the official exchange rate) by US estimates of Soviet GNP in US prices (for 1978). The highest figure is V.G. Treml's calculation (in principle, a more meaningful one) in terms of domestic rouble prices (Neuberger and Tyson 1980). But even the higher figures portray the USSR as relatively independent of foreign trade – as is usual with very large countries.

* The term Eastern Europe is used here to mean the smaller European members of the Council for Mutual Economic Assistance (CMEA): Bulgaria, Czechoslovakia, the German Democratic Republic, Hungary, Poland and Romania.

The country and commodity composition of Soviet trade

The USSR is a country which, despite its moderate to high level of industrialisation, has a strong emphasis on fuel and raw materials in its exports, and on machinery and manufactured consumer goods (and also food) in its imports. This is illustrated in Table 6.3 (see p. 109). (The figures, in fact, understate the predominance of primary products in Soviet exports; the USSR is the world's second largest gold producer, and a major exporter of non-monetary gold, but gold sales are not included in the export figures.)

This distinctive pattern stems from a combination of 'traditional' comparative advantage (relatively very rich natural resource endowment) and systemic comparative disadvantage (the system is relatively weak in farming and in the introduction of new technology, the attainment of quality in manufactures, and in marketing). At the same time, the commodity composition of Soviet trade is very much affected by the differences between groups of trade partners. The USSR trades on a different basis with different partners, and it is important to consider in turn its trading activities with different groups of countries.

There are two different ways of looking at the country composition of Soviet trade.

(i) *Politico–economic groupings*: socialist (of which, CMEA); developed capitalist; developing countries. This is the way Soviet trade returns are split up. For 1980 the corresponding percentages of total merchandise trade turnover were 53.7 (48.6); 33.6; 12.7.

(ii) *Financial groups*: barter/bilateral/'soft currency' trade (of which CMEA is a large part, but which also includes Finland and some developing countries); hard/convertible currency/multilateral settlement trade (the West and some developing countries). These financial groupings are important, and will be explained more fully.

Bilateral trade means, fundamentally, trade in which settlement is by the mutual balancing of two-way total flows of goods and services. The two parties usually aim at a balance each year with any eventual end-year imbalance to be offset by an imbalance in the opposite direction next year. This method of settlement applies to about three-fifths of Soviet trade. In general, there is no money settlement between bilateral trade partners. This sort of arrangement, like any form of barter, tends to limit the volume of transactions, in comparison with what would be achieved with the use of money. Prices tend to be specially negotiated with each bilateral trade partner.

Multilateral trade, on the other hand, is trade in which imbalances are settled in convertible currencies or gold. The attainment of a two-way balance with each trade partner is not necessary. This form of settlement is mainly with the West; it allows Soviet sterling surpluses, for example, to offset Deutschmark deficits, and so on. Such trade is generally at world prices. Important in Soviet transactions, but not shown in Soviet country-by-country trade returns, are arms sales for convertible currency. In multilateral trade in services, Soviet net earnings from shipping and tourism are also significant. Credit can more readily be introduced into a multilateral settlement system than into a bilateral system. This is almost a corollary of multilateralism, since such a system entails the use of internationally acceptable currencies, and these are acceptable as a means of deferred payment as well as in immediate settlement.

The importance of convertibility and its link with the system
Soviet-type economies have been called (by the American economist Joseph Berliner) 'documonetary' economies. This apt coinage conveys the fact that money alone is not sufficient, outside retail purchases, to provide a claim on available goods or resources. A plan allocation (usually entailing a document showing entitlement to supplies) is also needed. In this sense the rouble is not fully convertible into goods even within the USSR; it does not fulfil all the traditional functions of money. The rouble is still less of a genuine form of money for foreigners – to whom the allocation of goods does not extend. So *a fortiori* a Soviet-type economy has 'goods inconvertibility' so far as outsiders are concerned. Its money could not give them a claim on its resources. Foreigners therefore will not wish to hold it unless they can use it for another purpose, e.g. as a 'vehicle' currency for transferring assets into and out of other national currencies. The rouble could be made to serve this latter purpose if it were to be given external purely financial convertibility. In any case the rouble could not, in the very nature of the Soviet economic system, acquire external 'goods convertibility'.

In practice the Soviet authorities have not attempted to imbue the rouble with external convertibility of any kind. In other words, they do not intervene to support an official parity in foreign exchange markets. In fact they do not, officially, allow roubles to leave the country. The rouble is thus a purely domestic currency. The official exchange rate is therefore 'artificial' in the sense that there are no market pressures (buying and selling of roubles for other currencies) tending to push the exchange rate towards a level which relates the domestic purchasing power of the rouble over tradeable goods to the purchasing power of other countries over tradeable goods.

A further consequence of these arrangements is that the rouble, unlike convertible currencies in the Western world, does not link domestic to world prices. It is perfectly possible for a Soviet car to be sold domestically at several times the official rouble equivalent of its export price. In general, the structure of domestic prices diverges sharply from that of foreign trade prices. As a result the rouble values assigned to foreign transactions are said to be in 'foreign trade roubles'. These are merely a unit of account, not a currency in which any settlements are made, and they differ from the domestic rouble. The Hungarian forint is about to be made convertible; otherwise what has been said here about the rouble applies also to the other CMEA currencies.

In bilateral trade with other Soviet-type economies, the prices used are supposed to reflect world (i.e. approximately, Western) prices, but are adjusted by negotiation and influenced by the need to arrive at mutually balancing total flows. Intra-CMEA prices are now adjusted annually on the basis of 'world' averages for the preceding five years. Up to 1975 they were adjusted only every five years.

Foreign trade planning
Merchandise and services imports are administratively determined by the central authorities (Gosplan, Ministry of Foreign Trade, Gosbank and the Foreign Trade Bank) in the light of bilateral agreements, hard currency and credit availability and gaps in domestic requirements. In turn, merchandise and services exports are planned to meet the requirements of the import bill (allowing for credit). From year to year, however, the decisions are for the most part a matter of marginal adjustment to previous flows, so established markets, customers and suppliers experience considerable continuity.

The central authorities face strong pressure from below (branch ministries, enterprises) for additional imports, especially of producer goods. Producers with soft budget constraints,* who are hoarders of inputs generally, press for foreign (especially Western) machinery, components and supplies because of the prestige, quality, technical sophistication, supply reliability, etc., associated with them.

On the other hand, they face export constraints 'from below' insofar as special bonuses for export production (including mark-ups of as much as 40 per cent on wholesale prices of machinery) are not sufficient apparently to make the meeting of world-market quality, delivery, servicing conditions attractive. So the 'system' is simultaneously trade-averse (exports) and trade-biased (imports).

Soviet economic dealings with other countries are affected by a circumstance that is stressed, as a rule, less than it should be. Most countries have flows of goods, services, labour and risk capital between

* The term 'soft budget constraints' comes from the Hungarian economist, János Kornai. He considers enterprises which can rely on subsidies from a higher authority to avert any threat of closure or significant reduction of operations to have 'soft' budget constraints; enterprises which face real threats of bankruptcy or significant redundancies or both have 'hard' budget constraints. Soft budget constraints operate mainly, but not exclusively, in publicly-owned enterprises. Profoundly different patterns of behaviour result from the two sorts of budget constraints.

them. The USSR has virtually no migration and no inwards risk capital flows (equity investment from abroad is not allowed). Thus various kinds of contacts and transactions which are important (especially to technology transfer) between Western countries do not operate between the USSR and the outside world. A certain amount of borrowing from the West does occur, but it is very small in relation to Soviet investment. Nonetheless, the burden of financial adjustment to imbalances in goods and services transactions falls mainly on such borrowing. Neither emigrants' remittances from abroad, nor direct or portfolio investments from abroad are available to play the role which they play in some countries' balances of payments.

In this connection it should be noted that Soviet official data cover merchandise trade only. Gold sales are excluded; arms sales are apparently included in the total but not allocated between trade partners. Therefore all balance of payments figures (as distinct from balance of merchandise trade figures) are Western estimates. These estimates necessarily have a large margin of error, and our understanding of what the Soviet foreign trade planners are up to is to that extent impeded.

Policies: Soviet foreign trade as an eternal triangle

Trade with developing countries (c. one-eighth of the total) and with non-European-CMEA socialist countries (also c. one-eighth of the total) will be left to one side for the moment. The rest of Soviet trade, and the main policy choices about it, can be seen as a triangle: USSR–Eastern Europe–West. In 1980 Eastern Europe accounted for 42.5 per cent and the West for 33.6 per cent of Soviet merchandise trade turnover. Thus Soviet trade with the rest of the industrial world is about three-quarters of total Soviet trade, and has lately been split fairly evenly between the two groups. There are different rules of the game for Soviet trade with Eastern Europe and with the West, as was indicated at the beginning of this chapter. By the same token, different political and economic trade-offs are involved.

Trade with Eastern Europe

The USSR supplies critical amounts of energy to most of Eastern Europe, as the following figures indicate.

Table 6.1   Energy imports from USSR as percentage of total energy consumption, 1977

Bulgaria	70	Hungary	44
Czechoslovakia	35	Poland	15
GDR	28	Romania	2
		Total, EE6: 26	

Source: US CIA 1979: 11–12

These are 'hard' goods, in CMEA parlance, in that (i) they could be readily sold elsewhere for hard currency; and (ii) at prevailing CMEA prices, intra-CMEA demand for them exceeds intra-CMEA supply. By and large, (i) and (ii) go together. The USSR also supplies important raw materials (e.g. iron ore) which are also 'hard' goods. In return, the USSR gets mainly machinery, food and consumer goods. The machinery comes mostly into the 'soft goods' category (quality tends to be below world-market levels); the manufactured consumer goods partly so; the food is mostly 'hard'.

The terms of trade tended to move in favour of Eastern Europe and against the USSR in the 1960s and early 1970s; since intra-CMEA manufactures prices tended to rise more than intra-CMEA materials and energy prices. (This has to do with the greater scope for fudging the link with so-called 'world prices' in the case of highly heterogeneous manufactures than in the case of relatively homogeneous energy products and materials. It also may have something to do with greater knowledge of world-market prices on the part of the officials of the smaller East European countries, and their bargaining skills.) Meanwhile relative price movements on world markets tended to be somewhat more favourable to the USSR.

As a result:

(i) The opportunity cost for the USSR of trading with Eastern Europe rather than with the West tended to rise.

(ii) Correspondingly, the attractions for Eastern Europe of trading with the USSR, relatively to trading with the rest of the world, tended to increase. (This is not to say that increased trade with the West was not also attractive and, towards the end of the period, increasingly facilitated by improved political relations; merely that relative prices tended to move in the other direction.)

(iii) There *may* even have been absolute losses from CMEA trade for the USSR. Some estimates indicate that the average Soviet domestic cost of producing the exports needed to obtain 1,000 roubles' worth of imports from Eastern Europe may have exceeded the cost of Soviet domestic production of the same quantity of the same bundle of products as those imported. (Serious problems of method and interpretation are involved in this assessment. Different conclusions were reached in the early 1970s by C. H. McMillan and S. Rosefielde (see Gardner 1979: 1–14).

Even if (iii) could be shown not to have been true, it remains true that the USSR could have benefited from some switching of trade from Eastern Europe to the West. The 1973–4 and 1979–80 oil price jumps exacerbated this problem. The USSR responded by pushing through new CMEA price rules from the end of 1974, and managed to improve its net barter terms of trade with other CMEA countries by 26 per cent between 1970 and 1980 (Soviet official data). But even so, in 1980

Soviet oil was about half the price of OPEC oil to Eastern Europe. Has Eastern Europe, then, been 'exploiting' the USSR? Not necessarily.

(i) We need to distinguish between medium-term (less than 10 years) and long-term effects. In the long term, by forcing Eastern Europe to trade mainly with the USSR, rather than the West and to restrict movements of people and risk capital between Eastern Europe and the West, Moscow's pressures tended to cut Eastern Europe off from sources of technological improvement and from competitive market pressures for high product quality. As a long-run constraint, this has hampered the growth of productivity and prosperity in, at least, the initially more advanced East European countries (Czechoslovakia, East Germany, perhaps to some extent Hungary and Poland). On the other hand, by pushing through Soviet-type industrialisation, the Moscow connection may, on balance, have promoted productivity growth in the less developed East European countries. (For example, it is impossible to say whether the Romanian people would have fared better or worse than they have if Romania had been left as a peripheral late-developing European capitalist country.)

(ii) If Soviet–East European trade was unfavourable, in respect of prices, to Moscow, there may still have been *quantity* decisions which were more favourable to the USSR. The present severe constraint on the quantity of Soviet oil and gas going to Eastern Europe – no increase in oil supplies above 1980 levels – is one example.

(iii) The political alignment of Eastern Europe has been secured by heavy dependence on Soviet energy and materials, as well as by Soviet troops.

All the same, Moscow was trying to move towards a larger 'Western' element in its trade up to about 1976, since Eastern Europe could not, for systemic reasons, meet its technology requirements as effectively as the West. (There are reports of machinery acquired in intra-CMEA trade being hard to 'place' with potential user factories.) To some extent the same can be said of food supplies. By the same token, Eastern Europe, despite its gains from CMEA trade, saw long-run gains from increased Western trade – mainly because of benefits from Western technology.

There were therefore pressures for some shift, at the margin, towards greater trade with the West. Such a shift should not be thought of as something that is entirely 'at the expense of' intra-CMEA trade. In the medium-to-long term, intra-CMEA trade could actually be boosted by East–West trade. Injections of Western technology have tended to raise output and therefore the scope for intra-CMEA trade. One conspicuous example is the intra-CMEA gas supplies through the Orenburg gas pipeline. These have been facilitated by the Western large-diameter pipe and compressor stations incorporated in that pipeline.

Trade with the West

For the USSR, the attractions of trade with the West have been indicated above. (The attraction, to trade officials, of travel in the West and access to Western goods and currencies, should also be borne in mind.) There have been six main costs or constraints.

(i) The difficulty of increasing exports to competitive hard currency markets, especially exports of manufactures. Soviet and East European shares of OECD imports have not significantly increased since 1970. For the USSR, however, the limited performance of exports to the West in terms of volume was offset in the 1970s by rising hard currency earnings from arms sales to developing countries and by windfall price gains for gold, oil, gas and other primary product exports. Thus energy accounted in the late 1970s for around half of hard currency merchandise exports. Even so, export performance limits imports from the West.

(ii) Increased contact with Westerners tends to undermine traditional Soviet discipline and orthodoxy. This worries the KGB and, probably, the Politburo.

(iii) Western governments had potentially more scope for commercial leverage (blackmail) for foreign policy purposes. This has not in fact worked very well for the West. The usual pattern of Western economic sanctions in the late 1970s amounted to saying: stop taking over Africa/Afghanistan, etc. or we will try very hard to agree amongst ourselves not to sell you chemical plants/gas pipelines/grain, etc. The lure of the next chemical plant/gas pipe/grain sale has always been too much for somebody. Business is then resumed as usual. But such threats have now been uttered sufficiently often and sanctions have perhaps had some sufficiently cost-raising and disruptive effects on the USSR to arouse fears of 'dependence' and worries about instability of supplies from the West (e.g. US grain supplies). The deterioration of Soviet–US relations after 1974 was crucial in dampening Soviet policy-makers' enthusiasm for East–West trade.

(iv) Several East European countries, less well able to cope with (i) than the USSR, got into severe hard currency debt problems in the mid-1970s. This impinged on Soviet creditworthiness. It may have made Soviet leaders decide that it was dangerous to raise Soviet indebtedness in case the credit rating of the whole CMEA group should fall sharply and endanger all future East–West trade.

(v) The import of Western inflation, and increased vulnerability to Western macroinstability generally, has increasingly been seen as a threat. This was much less important to the USSR (because of its size) than to Eastern Europe, but the import of macroeconomic instability into Eastern Europe was itself enough to create worry for Moscow.

(vi) Limited Soviet output growth in key export items, especially oil,

Table 6.2 Shares of USSR trade turnover with socialist, Western and developing countries (per cent)

	1970	1971	1972	1973	1974	1975	1976	1977	1978	1979	1980
Socialist	65.2	65.4	65.5	58.5	54.1	56.3	55.6	57.3	59.8	56.1	53.7
of which:											
CMEA	55.6	56.2	59.6	54.0	48.9	51.8	50.8	52.5	55.7	51.9	48.6 (EE6 42.5)
West	21.3	21.5	22.6	26.6	31.3	31.3	32.9	29.6	28.1	32.1	33.6
Developing	13.5	13.1	12.9	14.9	14.6	11.5	11.5	13.1	12.1	11.8	12.7

Source Vneshnyaya 1981b.

led to increasingly hard choices between CMEA and Western trade. Hard currency settlements were introduced into intra-CMEA trade as a partial (and ideologically disturbing) solution: they accounted in the late 1970s for perhaps 10–15 per cent of intra-CMEA transactions (Lavigne 1980: 37–69, at 42–3).

Conclusions

Soviet semi-isolation from world trade has always been an economic handicap (partly self-imposed, partly dictated by the hostility of Western governments). Foregoing potential gains from trade (and from economic relations more broadly) with the West has adversely affected, in particular, the growth of Soviet prosperity and productivity. Such trade would have meant the introduction of new products and processes and the growth of domestic food supplies. Meanwhile trade with Eastern Europe has entailed (and continues to entail) certain burdens of empire.

Realisation of these facts grew among the Soviet policy-making élites in the post-Stalin era and led to a growing involvement in trade with the West from the mid-1950s. This accelerated with the Nixon–Brezhnev détente of the early 1970s. (The development of Soviet official attitudes and institutions is described in Hanson 1981, Chapters 5 and 6.)

The OPEC price shocks of 1973–4 increased the USSR's burdens of empire in its trade with Eastern Europe, and to that extent promoted the search for closer trade links with the West. But at the same time, these shocks to the world economy precipitated a Western recession and stagflation which in many respects hindered the development of East–West trade. Soon after, international political developments led

Table 6.3 Broad commodity composition of Soviet merchandise trade, 1980 (per cent)

	Exports	Imports
Machinery, transport equipment	15.8	33.9
Fuel and energy	46.9	3.0
Ores, concentrates, metals	5.7	5.0
Steel rolling mill products and pipes	3.1	5.8
Chemicals	3.3	5.3
Timber, wood, paper	4.1	2.0
Textiles	1.9	2.2
Food and food materials	1.9	24.2
Manufactured consumer goods	2.5	12.1
Other	14.8	6.5

Source Vneshnyaya 1981a: 18–19, 32.

to a more hostile and precarious relationship between Washington and Moscow.

In these circumstances Soviet policy-makers drew back from the pursuit of increased Western trade. In particular, orders for Western machinery have fallen since 1976, and remained relatively low. (Reported orders totalled about US$6 billion in 1976 and were at an annual rate varying between US$2.5–4 billion in 1977–81.) Present indications are that this retreat to traditional Russian/Soviet isolationism is likely to continue, though without a complete return to the minimisation of East–West trade of the Stalin era. In the Soviet Eleventh Five Year Plan (1981–5), total trade volume is supposed to increase at 4.1 per cent p.a.; CMEA trade 5.6 per cent p.a.; non-CMEA trade 2.3 per cent (*Pravda*, 20 November 1981). By contrast, in 1970–80 Soviet exports to CMEA rose at 4.9 per cent p.a. (volume) and imports at 6.3 per cent p.a., while export volume to non-socialist countries rose at 7.1 per cent p.a. and import volume at 11.4 per cent p.a. (*Vneshnyaya* 1981a). The sparse published plan figures for foreign trade have in the recent past understated the growth of Soviet–Western relatively to Soviet–East European trade (in comparison with the outcome). It would therefore be premature to conclude that these figures tell us what the Soviet planners will actually do. The apparent emphasis on CMEA trade, however, corresponds with the views now commonly expressed in the Soviet press, in which the costs and defects of trade with the West have lately been stressed. An improvement in East–West political relations now looks a necessary condition of any return to a strong growth in the volume of Soviet–Western trade. And even an improvement of this sort would do only a little to weaken the constraints on Soviet policy which the financial problems of Eastern Europe have created.

Nonetheless, the potential gains from trade with the West remain a considerable attraction for the makers of Soviet economic and trade policies. At the same time, the economic costs and constraints which Moscow faces in trade with Eastern Europe continue to exert a drag on CMEA transactions, and intra-CMEA trade could still benefit indirectly from growth in East–West trade. The Soviet leaders and planners cannot, in the near future, escape this particular set of economic and political dilemmas.

7 The Military Build-up
Jonathan Alford

In general usage, adjectival qualifications often dramatise the nature of change in the Soviet military establishment – 'massive', 'unprecedented', 'terrifying', 'unjustified' and 'brutal' are all words which spring to mind as preceding the words 'military build-up' in recent public statements by Western political leaders. That there has been upward change in both the quality and quantity of Soviet forces is generally true in all components of an already large and diverse capability. However, it is not the purpose of this chapter to chart that change in any detail. Nor is it the purpose of this chapter to be unduly polemical. To argue what is a Soviet initiative in this respect and what is a Soviet reaction to a Western military initiative is not particularly helpful. There seem to be elements of both in that interaction between East and West which is often inaccurately and simplistically called 'the arms race'.

The aim is altogether less complicated: it is simply to ask why the Soviet Union continues to invest massively in a military capability, at a time when most Soviet economic indicators are more or less adverse, when the Western threat seems not to be increasing (although Soviet perceptions may be different) and when common prudence might indicate, at the least, some diversion of scarce resources to the civil sector. In the absence of internally consistent Soviet statements of intent, much of what is said here is inferred from what little we know. For example the Soviet Union is unlikely to admit publicly the need to garrison adjacent states for fear of defection, yet there can be little doubt that at least one purpose of the Soviet army is to enforce loyalty in neighbours, where loyalty is suspect.

In writing about the Soviet Union and its external policy one can never quite escape the essentially circular discussion about intentions and capabilities nor can one ever categorically state that the Soviet military capability is not being acquired with the intention sooner or later of defeating the forces of the West in battle. Even without worst-case analysis, one has to admit that, given favourable circumstances, any Soviet leadership might decide to resolve the dispute between socialism and capitalism by force. On the other hand, a wholly benign interpretation of Soviet motives, concentrating exclusively on the defensive concerns of Soviet planners and the need to maintain internal order, has to come to terms with and explain certain things which only make sense in the context of a determination to change the correlation of forces in favour of the Soviet Union. It is, for example, hard to justify Soviet sea power on the basis of maritime interests; it is also hard to explain the exclusively offensive orientation of Soviet forces and Soviet doctrine; and it is hard to explain the changes in the Strategic Rocket Forces (SRF) in the direction of greater accuracy, variety, size and power except in the context of some desire, at the least, to overawe the United States.

What follows is based on certain very fundamental assumptions about the nature of the Soviet state and about the way that the Soviet leadership views the external world. This analysis takes it that the Soviet Union:

— desires to preserve the basic integrity of the Soviet state against its enemies;
— wishes progressively to change the 'correlation of forces' in the world in favour of the Soviet Union and to strengthen the forces of socialist transformation;
— understands very well the role of military power in international politics; and
— does not wish, in pursuit of its aims, to risk a nuclear war.

This hierarchy of underlying aims permits a more careful definition of what Soviet military power is for. It is defensive, in the sense of ensuring that no imaginable combination of adversaries should be able to threaten Soviet security, and military force can protect the gains of socialism abroad. It can also be offensive, in that the use or threatened use of military force can bring about, or help to bring about, socialist transformations in the external world. Yet these two words 'offensive' and 'defensive' become inconveniently blurred because the Soviet Union appears to believe, to use the old military cliché, that offence is the best form of defence. It has apparently no difficulty accepting that almost all threats to the state are ameliorated by the possession of a capacity to act preventively or pre-emptively against Soviet enemies. Using different language, the Soviet Union has acquired and is continuing to acquire military forces which effectively deny any exploitable military options to its enemies.

Taking Soviet security policy back to 1945, what one seems to observe is the Soviet Union chasing the chimera of absolute security, frustrated at many points by the American creation of security mechanisms or strategic weapon systems to deny them that sense of invulnerability. With each frustration, Soviet security policy twists and turns, unable to escape from the reality that *total* Soviet security, absence of danger to the USSR, can only be purchased at the expense of insecurity for virtually the rest of the world – which, for obvious reasons, the rest of the world is unable to accept. To have such a preclusive definition of security as this is not conducive to any system of international stability and balance, except on Soviet terms.

In this restless search for absolute security, the Soviet forces perform a number of different roles. The Soviet leadership, without perhaps knowing it, is distinctively Hobbesian in its view of the world, understanding well that 'reputation for power is power'. Perceptions of Soviet military power and widespread acknowledgement of its permanence can only induce extreme nervousness, divide opponents and cause social dislocation in those countries that believe themselves potentially threatened by it. The shadow of Soviet power falls over Soviet borderlands both to ensure that any hostile power is kept distant from the Soviet Union and to ensure compliant neighbours.

The armed forces also ensure that the Soviet Union is acknowledged to be the alternate superpower. It is generally accepted that in most of the dimensions of state power, the Soviet Union lags behind the United States, but, in writing the rules of the competition, the Soviet Union has chosen military power as the means of judging superpower status for, in that field at least, the Soviet Union has succeeded. It is not seriously in doubt that in quantity, and increasingly in quality, the Soviet armed forces qualify for superpower status, and it is likely that they will come increasingly to emphasise that role, given their relative failure in so many other fields.

Next, the Soviet army is certainly a socialising factor in the USSR, given the disparity of the Soviet population in ethnic and linguistic terms. While many would agree that the transmission of commands in Russian through a multilingual body is likely to be difficult and to detract from the overall performance of the military machine, the fact remains that compulsory service is a way of incorporating the minorities into one of the organs of the state, with a consequent appeal to a wider patriotism. It is not clear to what extent loyalty to the Soviet state now over-rides loyalty to the separate republics, but it is clear that the Soviet army, together with associated youth movements, is the chief means of breaking down barriers to a larger identity. Together with that linguistic and anti-ethnic purpose comes another which is more broadly educational. The introduction of the able-bodied male population to mechanical and, to a lesser extent, electrical and electronic skills in the services goes some way to make up for a general lack of mechanical aptitude, at least in rural areas.

Finally, there is also a circular quality in terms of the influence of the Soviet armed forces. Because they have been elevated so high in the pantheon of Soviet heroes, not only for past successes in war but also for present achievements, they have acquired an influence over the Soviet leadership which ensures that they will continue to gain whatever the military regard as an appropriate share of the cake. Moreover they appear to have gained a virtual monopoly on military information and so define the threats to the Soviet Union. It is indeed very hard to imagine, particularly during a succession struggle, that the military leadership will not get most of what they are demanding, even if that means starving other sectors of the economy of development and investment funds. This does not mean that the military are likely to be so irresponsible as to make demands that would bankrupt the state, but it does seem likely that, at a time of scarcity, the military will demand and achieve some sacrifice of living standards and public investment to ensure that an increasingly costly military establishment can be maintained and even marginally increased.

To suggest, as does the present American administration, that pressure on the civil economy will cause the leadership to cut back on military investment seems not to accord with political realities in the Soviet Union. Add to that the argument of serious economists that resources and plant are not easily diverted in the Soviet economic system from one sector to another (if 10 per cent of military funds were stopped, only one tenth of that might trickle across and then only after five years) and the prognosis is for little, if any, relaxation of Soviet military investment patterns.

Soviet doctrine, even setting aside the more obviously propagandistic statements, seems clearly to be directed to damage-limitation in war and that applies at least as much on the nuclear level as on the conventional. Without necessarily seeking war, there seems to be a general acknowledgement that war may come and that, if it does, the Soviet Union intends to ensure that, by striking at the sources of enemy power, the capacity of enemies to damage the Soviet Union is, so far as possible, neutralised. It sees no virtue in mutual vulnerability, preferring instead to strike pre-emptively at all military targets. In the Soviet mind-set, *any* reduction in an opponent's offensive capability is worth securing. Hence the Soviet Union has invested and continues to invest in large land-based intercontinental ballistic missiles (ICBMs) of increasing accuracy, in anti-submarine warfare and in air defences, while at the same time endeavouring to safeguard so far as is possible, its own nuclear systems against a first strike by the United States.

I believe that the primary justification for this investment remains the deterrence of the United States rather than the attainment of a disarming first-strike capacity of their own, for it seems unlikely that the Soviet military leadership believes that it can in fact limit damage to the Soviet Union to 'acceptable' levels, given the large and varied American strategic nuclear forces. Nevertheless, the Soviet leadership must be rather happy at the political consternation caused by the Western perception of the capabilities of Soviet strategic nuclear forces.

Turning to nuclear forces for primary employment in the theatre, that is against Western Europe and China, there are again obvious reasons for the Soviet Union to continue to invest in weapon systems of shorter range to cover targets closer to the Soviet Union. Originally it seems that there was a highly-developed notion of holding Western Europe hostage, when it was still not possible for the Soviet Union directly to threaten the continental United States. With the attainment of an intercontinental capability, it nevertheless remained necessary to neutralise the military targets in Western Europe and in China both because many of these were nuclear systems, particularly American nuclear systems forward-based in Europe, which threatened the Soviet Union. And also because, if there were to be a war in Europe which, for whatever reason, crossed the nuclear threshold, many targets of conventional military significance might be destroyed by nuclear means. Hence it was entirely logical for the Soviet Union initially to deploy large numbers of SS-4 and SS-5 shorter-range ballistic missiles in the 1960s, and to replace those, as the technology became available, with the more survivable and effective SS-20 missiles, together with a diverse establishment of nuclear-capable aircraft of considerable range, payload and penetrative ability.

The size and orientation of Soviet conventional forces is more problematic. Clearly one reason for the forward deployment of large numbers of Soviet forces in Eastern Europe has to do with the need to garrison the Soviet empire, but that does not adequately explain the exclusively offensive structure, doctrine and practising of these forces. For that one has, I believe, to look at geography and history. It is only necessary to assert that, given the length of Soviet borders, conventional defence of the USSR is impossible now, and that it has not proved possible in the past. In other words, if the Soviet Union is too large to be defensible in conventional terms, only preparations to conduct an offensive–defence make military sense. That means carrying the war on to an opponent's territory and there disrupting or destroying the means of conducting war. By seizing the initiative, by seeking to attain surprise and by employing the means, political as well as military, to dislocate an opponent's preparations for war, the Soviet Union might hope to unbalance an opponent and altogether remove the threat to the Soviet Union.

Extending that notion backwards into deterrence, the Soviet Union might hope that the threat of such action would deter any potential opponent from preparing to commit an aggressive act. The difficulty for the neighbours of the Soviet Union, as we are painfully aware, is that it is hard if not impossible to distinguish between a concept of deterrence by the threat of attack and preparations to attack. By here placing a somewhat benign interpretation on Soviet conventional preparations, it is possible to argue that intentions could change, if the Soviet Union came to believe that a conventional attack might succeed at modest cost, and that the Soviet Union is fully aware of the political dividends to be gained from the sense of unease that such a posture evokes in its neighbours. Large armies and air forces are, of course, natural for the Soviet Union, but they do not seem preternaturally large, given the size of the Soviet Union, its population, its poor internal communications and its multiplicity of potential opponents. Nor does it seem unnatural that it should seek to improve the quality of its equipment in a world that it, by its own ideology, must regard as hostile. Nevertheless, the consequences of this conventional investment and massive capability to mobilize Soviet reserves are such as to force those countries on the Soviet periphery to take prudent measures to guard against the possibility of change in Soviet intentions and that in turn, in the absence of durable political arrangements, can be used to justify further military investment in the Soviet Union.

The fourth general area of Soviet activity is more distant from the Soviet Union and concerns both maritime and power projection capabilities. This activity is certainly harder to explain, given that the Soviet Union is a supremely continental power whose overseas interests are at best marginal in terms of national security. It can be approached at three levels: the psychological; the defensive; and the offensive.

When the Kaiser was asked why Germany, another continental power, needed a navy, he is believed to have replied, 'for general purposes of greatness', and that, at the first level of analysis, goes a long way to explain the growth of the Soviet navy over the past two decades. In fact, it has not been a growth in terms of absolute numbers, for the Soviet navy, although previously a coastal navy, has been for very many years extremely numerous. It has rather been a growth in long-range power and visibility. It is the general impressiveness of Soviet ships which, as Admiral Gorshkov presumably intended, has attracted notice. They now operate in distant waters and are available to support Soviet state policy in the Third World. In short, the USSR now uses its navy to support Soviet diplomacy as the United States (and Britain before it) has used its navy. In fighting his bureaucratic battles for funds for the navy, Admiral Gorshkov appears to have used some very traditional 'great power' arguments to support his case, including demands for equal rights and equal access.

At the second level – defensive – the Soviet Union needs powerful (primarily submarine) forces to threaten American carrier groups, which can in turn threaten the Soviet homeland, and anti-submarine forces both to neutralise American fleet ballistic missile submarines and protect Soviet ballistic missile submarines from attack by American 'hunter–killer' nuclear-powered submarines. Given the state of Soviet anti-submarine warfare (ASW) technology, it is far from clear that the Soviet navy can do much to neutralise US SSBNs, but they would, in accordance with doctrine, continue to try to do so.

At the third level – offensive – the Soviet Union is aware of a general Western vulnerability to the interdiction of supply and reinforcement routes. Not to play upon that vulnerability in war would, in Soviet eyes, be a ludicrous failure to apply the principles of strategy. Again it would be primarily nuclear-powered submarines, but backed this time by land-based air power, that would be the instrument for interdiction. But also under this sub-head should fall Soviet land and air power projection capabilities to support or extend distant Soviet interests, coupled with an aggressive policy with respect to arms transfers.

In a necessarily brief chapter, one can do no more than assert that the somewhat more adventurous policy pursued by the Soviet Union with respect to the Third World has been facilitated by a growing ability to project power rapidly into distant areas. Soviet airborne divisions, a large carrying capacity easily diverted from the 'civil' air and mercantile fleets, and a stockpile of weapons available for rapid transfer all tend to support Soviet policy. There is at least a *prima facie* case that this adventurousness stems from an understanding both of American retrenchment in the 1970s and the utility of particular kinds of force projected either by the Soviet Union itself or by proxies, with the aim both of holding off American competitive intervention and effecting a radical transformation of local circumstances.

All of this – whether rockets, aircraft, tanks or ships – is of course the product of Soviet industry, and what is remarkable is not so much the aggregate output but the fact that the defence sector of Soviet industry seems to perform so much better than other sectors. That in turn implies that very high priorities for the available skills and materials are accorded to the defence sector, to the obvious detriment of other sectors. What is also clear is that this investment is not readily or rapidly transferable to other purposes and most observers tend to remark on the inflexibility of Soviet economic planning machinery. Having created this impressive military production machine which functions (at least in comparison with other sectors) with moderate efficiency, it is simply very difficult to turn it off again. Norms are set and plans are met almost regardless of need. Inertia plus the political clout of the military is a combination likely to ensure the continued production of new arms for both the armed forces of the state and as an important foreign currency earner in the export markets.

How much money the Soviet Union really invests in the armed forces of the state is a legitimate subject for debate. The best answer is to state frankly that we do not know. There are no published figures to give a reliable guide and dollar/rouble cost comparisons are notoriously fallible. Given that manpower costs are remarkably low in comparison with Western figures, what is left for investment in research and development (R and D) procurement is proportionately much higher, and there is no way that what is currently procured can be procured cheaply. The least that can be said is that the sheer numbers of high quality equipments entering service at the present time must represent a substantially increased investment over earlier levels and that, if the trend continues while the overall economic performance remains unimpressive, this can only mean a progressive shift of resources into the military sector. There are, of course, four possible interpretations of this trend: first, it could be to achieve world domination by military conquest; second, it could demonstrate the hold of the military over the resource allocation process; third, it could be because the Soviet leadership has created a monster it can no longer effectively control; and fourth, it could be because the Soviet leadership labours under such an enduring, if mistaken, sense of threat that it feels it necessary to take even greater measures to provide security for the Soviet state. All are admissible and they are not mutually exclusive; they may even, under the circumstances surrounding the Soviet Union, be mutually reinforcing over the longer term and that, in the absence of any mutual understanding about détente, may prove to be the most worrying thing of all.

It should be clear from what has been said here that there are several competing explanations for the Soviet military build-up, ranging from the modestly benign to the distinctly malign. The simplistic version fails to convince: it is unlikely that the Soviet Union now or in the immediate future would see a military solution either in Western Europe or in the Far East as sufficiently free of appalling risk to constitute a realistic policy option. But nor does the benign interpretation of a Soviet reaction to external threat hold much water. It is not evident that the level of threat to the USSR has in fact changed much if at all with time. If anything, it has probably reduced and certainly did so in the 1970s under the impact of détente and American retrenchment after Vietnam, when US defence expenditures were actually reduced in real terms by 25 per cent. In short, there is little obvious correlation of any kind between external threat and Soviet levels of expenditure. What is worrying for the West is that the build-up appears to be almost, if not entirely, autonomous and independent of events in the outside world. Nor is the explanation of traditional Soviet overinsurance comforting in view of the ambiguous attitude of the Soviet military machine to the distinctions between offence and defence.

One is forced to conclude that there is a connection between change in the Soviet military structure and the desire to utilise the perception of disparities in the military balance for political ends. It is the shadow of

Soviet military power extending over the Soviet periphery to distant waters and non-contiguous areas that is intended to shape our view of what is politically feasible and ultimately to persuade us that accommodation over key issues with the Soviet Union is preferable to confrontation.

8 Soviet–East European Relations
George Schöpflin

The first principle of Soviet–East European relations is that this particular relationship is not to be confused with other forms of international and inter-state contact. There may be superficial similarities to the practice of international relations in other parts of the world, but the reality of Soviet–East European relations – East–East relations for short – is qualitatively different, and this difference is insisted upon by the Soviet Union in the corpus of doctrines called the Brezhnev doctrine. Hence, as a first proposition, the concept of state sovereignty, for example, does not apply to East–East relations.

The basis of that relationship must, therefore, be sought elsewhere. Here the central concept of significance is the Soviet conception of power and its derivative in this context, the Soviet concept of alliance. To oversimplify a lengthy argument, the essence of the Soviet (and before that, the Russian) concept of power is concentration. In this perspective, power should be centralised as far as possible and monopolised. And above all, the wise ruler acting by this precept will do everything to prevent the emergence of competing centres of power (Szűcs 1981). In the field of domestic politics, this has become the leading role of the party, the political monopoly of the communist party, which acts as the single legitimate political aggregator in the state and, indeed, seeks to merge with the state.

In international affairs, this aspiration to create a monopoly of power is not (yet) possible, but the frame of values which has had its domestic expression in the leading role doctrine infuses the international field as well. The essence of this is that the Soviet Union lacks a concept of alliance and only understands subordination. Subordination is thus a pragmatic substitute for the complete submergence of other interests, which is regarded as the ultimate aim of monopolising power. In official language, this is called the coming of full communism.

The post-war era of East–East relations is full of examples of the rejection of any real alliance with the East European states by the Soviet Union and on its insistence on subordination (Kende 1982). In Hungary in 1956, a viable compromise between Moscow and Budapest was feasible, had the Soviet Union been willing to accept that a neutral Hungary would remain within the Soviet orbit. Other crises of the system (Czechoslovakia in 1968, Poland in 1980–81) provide the same lesson. Once the Soviet Union had successfully extended its power over a particular state, even if it was later forced to dilute some of that power under de-Stalinisation, it would never abandon its control over that state. What is more, the Soviet leadership has never concealed this objective – it simply sought to legitimise its aspirations by camouflaging them in Marxist–Leninist language (Brzezinski 1967).

The nature of Soviet control over Eastern Europe

Control is not the same as coercion. Precisely because the Soviet leadership deploys power by its particular traditions of maximising it, the leadership has shown that it recognises that the greater the element of consensus in the exercise of power, the easier the task of exercising it becomes. If in the Stalinist period, power was exercised in Eastern Europe overwhelmingly through coercion, this changed gradually thereafter. The Soviet aim over the last 25 years has been to foster an ever-increasing group of beneficiaries and agents who would accept the legitimacy of Soviet overlordship in Eastern Europe and the legitimacy of the Soviet type of polity, even though this was widely regarded as an alien import. Hence within the East European élites, there is to be found a large class of people who see their interests as bound up with the Soviet Union and are, therefore, prepared to uphold the Soviet-type system.

This proposition can be shown to be viable by the case of Czechoslovakia in 1968, when a section of the élite took control of the Czechoslovak party and attempted to rearrange the political relationship between rulers and ruled. This was not sanctioned by the regulations of the Soviet monopolistic order, and the Soviet leadership felt it had to act to uphold that order. The threat of an autonomous Czechoslovak leadership, with its own sources of legitimacy separate from the Soviet connection and potentially in competition with it, was too great to tolerate. In a word, the more the Czechoslovak leadership declared that the Czechoslovak party had genuine popular support, the less the Soviet Union was inclined to recognise it as the kind of political organisation welcome in its area of monopoly. It is worth stressing that the doctrines of Marxism were quite irrelevant to this entire dispute, which was settled by reference to power.

This does draw attention to a significant aspect of the Soviet order, the existence of two tiers of control – a Soviet tier and an East European tier. The dependence, and hence weakness, of the latter is not necessarily regarded as a drawback by the Soviet Union, rather the contrary. Thus the Soviet Union will invariably prevent attempts to bring the East European political order into line with local traditions. Consequently, East European parties may be able to buy themselves limited popularity, but they will always remain alien. Their roots are alien, the communist revolution pushed through after the war was alien and their present system of rule is likewise alien. Again it is noteworthy that Yugoslavia, which has a ruling party with genuine native roots and with a good claim to have brought off a wholly domestic revolution, has been able to deviate markedly from the Soviet model.

As far as Soviet control over these East European parties is concerned, therefore, one can say that there exists an extensive degree of control (Gilberg 1981). Since at the end of the day these parties owe their existence and power to the Soviet Union, and to Soviet military might, this is perfectly understandable. In addition to that, there are other instruments of control in the international sphere that are significant. In the first place, there is the Warsaw Pact, and this is not simply the presence of given numbers of Soviet divisions in Poland, the German Democratic Republic (GDR), Czechoslovakia and in Hungary. (It is, incidentally, interesting that the most loyal ally of the Soviet Union, Bulgaria, does not need and certainly does not have Soviet troops on its soil.) This mechanism involves not merely the Warsaw Pact itself, but the network of mutual assistance treaties, which link the Soviet Union with every East European country, and every East European country with every other East European country. For what it is worth, if the Warsaw Pact were abolished tomorrow, it would not make all that much difference, because the underlying network to support this particular alliance system would remain in being. This is something which, incidentally, is absent in the West – NATO is not supported by this underlying structure (Dawisha in Dawisha and Hanson 1981).

The point of the Warsaw Pact is that it does perform a number of functions as a political organisation: it provides a forum for discussion at many levels of decision-making; at the very top, at the intermediate or Foreign Ministry levels and, perhaps most significantly, at the level of the army officer probably above the rank of colonel. These are people who go through a very similar training, a very similar process of socialisation, and the Soviets hope by this to develop the kind of military cadre who will be loyal to the Soviet Union and to the Soviet Union's variant of communism, to the extent of actually placing that loyalty higher than his loyalty to his own country, because he sees these loyalties as identical. This has actually arisen quite significantly in Poland, where it is not at all clear whether senior Polish officers – colonels and above – owe a primary loyalty to Poland or a primary loyalty to the Warsaw Pact (Jones 1981).

It is also worth discussing the Council for Mutual Economic Assistance (Comecon or CMEA) in this context, because in this instance one finds a form of control by means of a series of very low-level agreements, both bilateral and multilateral, among all the Comecon members, which link their economies with each other. This has been particularly important since the Complex Programme of 1970–71, which was supposed to introduce an intensification of this process. This does have a control function in as much as it subordinates the East European economies to that of the Soviet Union. In reality, there is probably more aspiration than achievement in this, largely because of the way in which the world economy has progressed since the 1970s, which has, in effect, intensified East European dependence on the West through imports of technology, investment, and so on. By the same token, that process reduced East European integration in Comecon.

Nevertheless one can see this effect, for example, in the crucial area of energy, (Poland excepted, for Poland is actually not energy dependent, having large stocks of coal) as far as the other East European countries, which are very poor in energy sources, are concerned. If the Soviet Union were to 'turn off the tap', notably in oil, but also natural gas, the East European economies would be in a very serious situation indeed. In such a hypothetical situation, the Hungarians would be in acute difficulties, as would the East Germans. Czechoslovakia would be somewhat less affected because it does have some domestic sources of coal and the switch from coal to oil has not been all that far-reaching. Romania still has domestic sources of energy, but these are insufficient to meet the demands of the massive oil-refining industry (mistakenly) built up in the 1970s. Bulgaria is similarly dependent on the Soviet Union. The Soviet–East European connection in the realm of energy is not only an example of economic control as it stands but, over the medium term, the relationship has contributed to a distortion of East European economic development patterns and helped to make these countries less efficient in world-marketing terms and thus more dependent on the Soviet Union.

For example, the continued supply of cheap energy to Hungary in the 1970s discouraged Hungarian planners from saving energy and helped to sustain the false belief that the era of cheap energy could be made to last well beyond the oil price explosion of the mid-1970s. Hungarians pressed on with their energy strategy, devised in the 1960s, and based on a profligate use of oil, simply because the pricing system was sending the wrong signals. Similarly, dependence on the Soviet market, encouraged by Comecon agreements, has perpetuated inefficiencies in East European industry, because the Soviet Union was capable of absorbing rather low-quality output; the point here is that goods manufactured for sale to the Soviet Union cannot be sold anywhere else. Furthermore, Soviet demand has concentrated on the machinery and equipment sector, with the result that several of the East European states have built up a strong machine manufacturing sector which has only one market, the Soviet Union. This obviously gives the latter considerable economic leverage.

The final area to be noted is a comparatively murky one. Here control is exercised through the so-called ideological co-operation treaties. (Treaties of ideological co-operation were signed in the early 1970s.) One might think it rather odd, in a way, that there are countries supposedly professing the same ideology, yet still needing ideological co-operation agreements. These are in all probability a framework for regular discussion by the party organisations on matters of mutual concern.

There was some suggestion that the impetus behind these treaties in the early 1970s was tied up with what has been called the Brezhnev Blueprint for the future of the communist world. This postulates that eventually, after a very long period of time, all education should be Sovietised. In other words, all education in Eastern Europe should be on the Soviet pattern, above all higher education, which, at the end of the day, would hasten the production of Soviet man and Soviet woman – the ultimate goal of communism, and the construction of socialism.

There is some evidence that this kind of co-operation is more intensive between Bulgaria and the Soviet Union. To a fair extent the Bulgarian University curriculum in some subjects has already been synchronised with the Soviet; in some fields, of course, the Bulgarians say it is simply not economic for Bulgaria to have departments in, say, nuclear physics. Therefore, all Bulgarians in this discipline will be trained in the Soviet Union. This is a process for which one can make out a very good case. It becomes rather more difficult when, say, there is a Polish or Czechoslovak research project in the social sciences. For example, this might deal with some area of class stratification. What then happens is that the participants find that before they can undertake their research, a Soviet comrade has to come along and supervise what they are doing. In this sort of area there is evidence that control is being extended. The other thing to be added to this is the training of large numbers of cadres, especially senior communist ones, in the Soviet Union. This is regarded as a way in which control is perpetuated. These people form an interest group, as they have all been through a kind of experience denied to, and distrusted by the rest of the population and that, therefore, sets them aside within the party machine. By the same token, they have much better links with the Soviet Union than perhaps other party cadres, and they already appear to form a very important network of interest within each East European party.

Eastern Europe as a source of instability

It has been a basic assumption in the argument hitherto that the populations of Eastern Europe would choose to change the existing political order if they had the freedom to do so. Consequently, the East

European regimes lack genuine legitimacy at the popular level, although they may enjoy it at the élite level. This, however, is too narrow a base for long-term stability, because whenever the morale of the élite is broken and that coincides with (and/or is partly occasioned by) popular unrest, the entire system is endangered. The Soviet Union will then intervene to restore the Soviet-type system. Crises of this kind have been comparatively rare in post-war Eastern Europe, even if they have occurred with greater frequency and intensity than the élites would like.

In the absence of a genuine, fundamental coincidence of mass and élite patterns, political stability must be based on other devices. Consumerism has been the most favoured – welfare benefits traded off against depoliticisation – and this has been extended by two other strategies. The élites have sought to portray themselves as national leaderships, and thus as guardians of the national identities of the polities over which they rule. This has had some success, but there will always be a conflict between East European nations and their subordination to the Soviet Union. At the same time, the channelling of nationalist resentment against non-Soviet targets (e.g. Hungary against Romania over Transylvania) is a highly dangerous strategem because it could potentially act on inter-state relations within Eastern Europe. This could oblige the Soviet Union to restore order at a high price.

The second set of concepts deployed to legitimate power is the portrayal of these parties as the sole repository of rationality in the polity and thus as the best fitted to exercise power. This runs counter to the everyday experience of Eastern Europe, where life is shot through with more inefficiency and incompetence than rationality. A significant aspect of this arises from the absence of popular control (necessitated by Soviet-type monopoly), which results in large-scale corruption and abuse of power. The party supposedly acts as its own control system and manifestly fails to do so – the example of Poland in the 1970s was only the most extreme. The élite simply uses public resources in a feudal manner, as if these were owned wholly by the élite, and rejects criticism as incompatible with the ruling monopoly. The system is sustained by the institution of the *nomenklatura*, the list of offices filled at the behest of the party throughout the state and also the list of those qualified to fill these posts (Voslensky 1980). This inevitably promotes political reliability over merit, and thus runs counter to efficiency and rationality.

The *nomenklatura* is a classic institution of the Soviet-type system and is a good example of the nature and imperatives of that system. On the one hand, it preserves a façade of pluralistic institutions and, on the other, it is a vital instrument for the concentration of power. It enables the party, both nationally and locally, to exercise control over a whole variety of institutions – from the judiciary to the fire service – efficiently and cheaply. The party thereby has access to patronage and can ensure loyalty. Internationally, *nomenklatura* exists *de facto* or *de jure* in the Soviet Union's control over senior appointments in East European countries. The size of the *nomenklatura* varies from country to country. In Poland, it grew enormously in the 1970s and reached down to factory foreman level. Whilst the *nomenklatura* system is excellent as an instrument of control, it works less well when the ruling élite places high emphasis on economic output, because political loyalty and optimal performance seldom go hand in hand, least of all in anti-risk monopolistic systems like those of East Europe. Hence there has been a tendency towards stultification and stagnation, which in turn undermine both rationality and efficiency.

The foregoing suggests strongly that the Soviet-type system can be sustained in times of economic prosperity, but that it encounters greater problems when there is a downturn, as was happening during the early 1980s. That did not automatically imply destabilisation in Eastern Europe. As long as the morale of the élites remained unbroken and as long as the legitimacy of the system was unaffected in their eyes, the system could be maintained. However, the cost of this maintenance appeared to be increasing. The passivity of the mass of the population could no longer be taken for granted when the instruments of pacification – higher consumption, low productivity – were wearing out. On the other hand, as seen, Eastern Europe is subjected to two tiers of control, and when the local tier was eroded in Poland in 1980–81, the Soviet Union was prepared to pay the cost of restoration. This implied a medium-term outlook of some fragmentation in Eastern Europe which would be glued together by the Soviet Union. The possibility of the Soviet Union itself becoming infected by the weakness in Eastern Europe appeared remote.

Whilst in Eastern Europe the system was manifestly performing badly, in the Soviet Union it continued to function to the satisfaction of both the élite and the masses, not least because in the Soviet Union the Soviet system was not alien but had developed from authentic, native roots. Hence, as long as the Soviet leadership's will to rule in Eastern Europe by its particular lights – sustaining the monopoly of power – remained in being, there was no hint that there might be any resentment of the mounting cost of running this empire. The Brezhnev doctrine, the formal justification of the Soviet Union's right to intervene in Eastern Europe, had not been abrogated and as the 1980s were under way, there were no indications of any readiness on the part of the Soviet Union to contemplate changes in the East–East relationship.

The instruments of coercion

With the assumption of power by the military in Poland, a new phase of communist politics can be said to have begun. This phase is, however, a logical outgrowth of the previous one and should not be seen as a caesura, except in terms of ideological rhetoric. The armed forces' putsch in Poland was not predicted because of the strong ideological inhibition on the political role of the military in communist states and the absence of a precedent from which to make predictions; once the inhibition was removed, the intervention did not appear illogical. In any polity, the disintegration of the civilian élite, as in the case of Poland, makes it likelier for the most disciplined force in society to mount an intervention. In Poland, this likelihood was reinforced by the higher value placed on monopoly of power than on political rationality, which would have involved a more equal relationship between rulers and ruled. As the Polish party disintegrated, the Soviet Union turned to the Polish armed forces to restore the monopoly, something which the armed forces were only too ready to do, given the similarity of values between communist rationality and organisation and military discipline (Checinski 1982a and b, Jones 1981).

At the same time, the putsch initially meant a total defeat for the remnants of the communist party, which was simply elbowed out of the way. By late 1982, the outcome of the putsch was unclear: the armed forces had entrenched themselves in various areas of power and administration, but the remaining fragments of the civilian élite were not ready to yield up all power and privileges without a struggle. Hence the putsch had failed to bring about the restoration of the *status quo ante*, the re-monopolisation of power in the hands of a single, homogeneous élite, with one line of command; on the other hand, it achieved its other objective of once more excluding society from participating in politics.

A repetition of the Polish experience is, therefore, only likely if the conditions which precipitated the coup – the collapse of civilian power and an upsurge of pressure from below – are reproduced. In the early 1980s, only Romania looked like a candidate for this fate, as Ceauşescu concentrated power in the hands of his extended family – replacing the clientilism of the communist party with that of the Ceauşescu family – and the country was caught in the grips of an advanced economic crisis. Through concentration of power in his own hands, the Ceauşescu system looked unlikely to survive its progenitor. But other than by death or assassination or palace coup – none of them events easy to predict – there was no way in which change could be effected in Romania. Furthermore, the Polish example could even give rise to a greater determination on the part of the other ruling élites to avoid the fate of their Polish *confrères*. They might well seek to re-impose discipline over excessive misuse of power and to retain control over their armed forces.

In this connection, the role of the secret police bears extra investigation, despite the paucity of information. Even in the Polish case, the secret police played a more significant role in the preparation and execution of the coup than appeared at first sight and continued to be one of the semi-independent contenders for power in the months that followed. Secret police forces are a crucial factor not only in the relationship between the local élite and the population but also in East–East relations. The secret police acts as a separate control mechanism in Eastern Europe and is much more closely supervised by the Soviet Union, despite de-Stalinisation. When the interests of the Soviet Union and the local élite run together, there will be no occasion for conflict. When a local élite collapses, the secret police remains one of the bedrocks of Soviet power. At the same time, these forces are also the party's private army and have a vested interest in the survival of communist rule as the best guarantor of their own existence. Popular fury was vented on the secret police in the Hungarian revolution, and its powers were under attack from Solidarity in Poland. The interdependence between the party and the secret police is close and the latter probably enjoys considerable independence, at any rate in its own budgets. Throughout the 1970s, Ministry of Interior budgets grew apace in Poland, Hungary and the GDR, suggesting rises in wage funds or an increasing number of employees.

Conclusion

The political structure of Eastern Europe appears less and less adequate to the political needs of these polities. Attempts to bring them up to date founder on Soviet imperatives. This implies that the political future of Eastern Europe is beset with uncertainties. Some of these may well be resolved with the advent of a new leadership in the Soviet Union with the will to launch new initiatives in the realm of East–East relations. But to judge from the history of those relations and the patterns of Soviet power, there is little to suggest that any Soviet leadership will be prepared to accept a qualitative transformation of that relationship, of the kind necessary for a genuine stabilisation of Eastern Europe on the basis of its own political traditions (Szporluk 1976).

The implication of this analysis, therefore, is that Eastern Europe may well continue as a source of instability for the Soviet system, but that those instabilities will not be seen as serious enough to warrant major readjustments. The Soviet Union, by reason of its approach to power, will continue to regard the concentration of power as of paramount value and will not shrink from paying the costs.

9 Sino–Soviet Relations*
Christina Holmes

The Sino–Soviet dispute existed long before it burst upon the world with the Amur–Ussuri border clashes of March 1969. What has been generally regarded as a 20-year period of friendship and co-operation between the most powerful and the most populous communist power was in fact a period of uneasy alliance. Chinese leaders resented Soviet high-handedness and discovered early on that Soviet 'aid' was in fact little more than normal bilateral trade. Peking paid in full, with interest, for instance, for the war materials supplied by the Soviet side during the Korean war.

Since 1969, when Soviet and Chinese troops fought over Zhenbao/Damansky Island, with over 800 Chinese and 40 Soviet casualties, Soviet leaders have regarded Peking as a serious threat to Soviet security and have sought the best means of containing that threat. Troops and military facilities along the 6,000 kilometre border with the People's Republic of China (PRC) have been reinforced and a new railway – the BAM – has been constructed to the north of the vulnerable Trans-Siberian line. There is evidence that Moscow at one time considered a pre-emptive strike against China, and diplomatic overtures aimed at improving relations with the PRC have been a consistent element of Soviet foreign policy (Kissinger 1979, 1982).

This split in the Communist ranks has been of tremendous strategic significance. Fear of the Marxist–Maoist monolith had fuelled McCarthyism in the United States during the 1950s. The demise of the monolith provided a catalyst for East–West détente in the early 1970s. The secret meetings between Henry Kissinger and top Chinese leaders, and the subsequent meeting between President Richard Nixon and Chairman Mao Zedong, paved the way for normalisation of Sino–American relations. Sino–Soviet competition for influence in the Third World led to proxy clashes between the two sides and a proliferation of new alignments.

The consensus among Western leaders and analysts is that the Sino–Soviet dispute was a windfall for the West. There seems now to be an assumption that Sino–Soviet *rapprochement* would be equally

* I would like to take this opportunity to express my sincere thanks to the Librarian and staff of the Press Library at Chatham House.

momentous in undermining Western security interests. Thus there is tremendous interest in every little event, overture and signal between Peking and Moscow. Quite naturally, one of the questions to be raised is whether the new Soviet leadership will lead to changes in Soviet policy toward China and in the Sino–Soviet relationship. In addressing this question we need to look at the history of the relationship, the nature of current Sino–Soviet differences and Soviet and Chinese perceptions.

An historical analysis reveals several changing and several constant elements affecting the Sino–Soviet dispute. As noted above, tensions existed between Peking and Moscow even in the immediate aftermath of the conclusion of the Sino–Soviet Treaty of Friendship, Alliance and Mutual Assistance in Moscow on 14 February 1950. Even the treaty negotiations had been frequently acrimonious, requiring Mao's presence in Moscow over a period of three months. Having defeated the Japanese 'imperialists' and seen the backs of the forces which had partitioned China, Mao was determined that the new People's Republic of China should be treated as an equal on the world stage. Some would say that the roots of the dispute lay even further back, in the pillage and plunder of the Mongol hordes, in the gradual encroachment of Russian explorers, hunters and trappers, in the 'unequal treaties' forced on the Chinese by the Russian tsars, and later in Stalin's decision to aid Nationalist forces in China from 1921 to 1949 instead of the struggling Communists. This legacy of hostility and suspicion cannot be ignored, but accepting that legacy as given, it is the period from 1950 to the present and into the future with which we are concerned here.

In the period to 1976, Sino–Soviet relations were plagued by state-to-state (national interests) and ideological (party-to-party) differences and by personal clashes between Soviet and Chinese leaders. One of the most serious of the state-to-state or practical differences between Moscow and Peking has already been alluded to – the Chinese realisation over time, and especially in the aftermath of the Korean War, that Soviet 'aid' was no more than trade and came with strings attached. Soviet leaders, on the other hand, began to decry Chinese ingratitude, and have since attempted to show the benevolent extent of Soviet assistance (Borisov and Koloskov 1975). In 1960, however, all Soviet and East European experts were withdrawn from China and blueprints for their projects destroyed. There followed in China the 'two terrible years' of severe economic hardship and famine.

Chinese leaders during the late 1950s and early 1960s were also beginning to question the reliability of the Soviet Union as an ally. Moscow had declined to provide a sample atomic bomb or the technology necessary for the production of nuclear weapons and refused to use its military or diplomatic power to support China in its 1958 attempt to gain control of Taiwan and in its border dispute with India in 1962. The Kremlin was also seen as unwilling to use its might in furtherance of the aims of the international communist movement and as bent on appeasing the imperialist powers by signing the Nuclear Test Ban Treaty in July 1963. To Soviet leaders, who had decided by the early 1960s to improve relations with the West, China came to appear as a liability in security terms, both reckless in support of its own interests and unrealistic in terms of what the Soviet Union could achieve internationally.

The territorial issue, one of the most problematic of the state-to-state differences, became public in the polemic following Khrushchev's agreement to remove Soviet missiles from Cuba in 1962. In their reply to a speech by Khrushchev, in which he taunted Mao, Chinese leaders on 8 March 1963 listed the 'unequal treaties' imposed on China by tsarist Russia. From that time they have consistently demanded that Soviet leaders acknowledge the 'unequal' nature of the 19th century treaties which established the frontier between the two states. Sino–Soviet border negotiations were begun in 1964, but Moscow refused to recognise the previous treaties as unequal, even though Peking renounced any claim to the more than one and a half million square kilometers of Chinese territory annexed by the tsars and stated its willingness to solve the border issue on the basis of those treaties. This has remained one of the more serious stumbling blocks in the border negotiations, which were resumed in the aftermath of the fighting in 1969.

An additional problem since then has been the insistance by Chinese leaders that Soviet and Chinese forces withdraw from all disputed areas along the border, i.e. areas where the boundary line was drawn in a different way in the maps exchanged between the two sides during the Sino–Soviet negotiations in 1964. Soviet leaders have insisted on a settlement of the boundary question on the basis of what they call the 'historically formed' and 'actually guarded' line. They further argue that Lenin's decrees in 1919 had, in fact, cancelled all unequal treaties, and that these were those dealing with rights of extra-territoriality and consular jurisdiction, concessions on Chinese territory, and the Russian share of indemnities imposed by imperialist countries on China after the suppression of the Boxer Rising, not those establishing the Sino–Soviet frontier (Keesing's Contemporary Archives 23641–5).

Ideological or party-to-party differences between China and the Soviet Union included differences over the proper way to handle 'contradictions' within the party and between parties, differences about the most appropriate lines of development toward the stage of full communism, and differences regarding relations with capitalist countries. I prefer to refer to these as 'ideological' rather than 'party-to-party' differences since relations between the two parties were severed in the mid-1960s. Chinese leaders date the beginning of the Sino–Soviet dispute from the 20th CPSU Congress held in Moscow in February 1956, where Nikita Khrushchev, then First Secretary of the CPSU, denounced Stalin in his concluding 'secret' speech. The Chinese and other party leaders had not been consulted or warned in advance and Peking feared that confusion would result from such bitter criticism of a former leader. The crises in Poland and Hungary in the summer and autumn of 1956 seemed to prove such fears justified and underlined the fact that the 20th Party Congress was a watershed in communist relations.

Chinese leaders also disapproved of the open Soviet criticisms of 'fraternal' parties – first of the Albanian party and then, at the Third Congress of the Romanian Workers' Party in Bucharest in June 1960, of the Communist Party of China (CPC) itself. They protested that Khrushchev had violated the principle of settling questions of common concern 'by consultation among the fraternal parties'. In the summer of 1961, the Soviet Union and some East European countries imposed economic sanctions on Albania, while China stepped up its economic aid.

In August 1968, the Kremlin went one step further in using its armed forces against those of a fraternal socialist state. The invasion of Czechoslovakia and the subsequent enunciation of the Brezhnev doctrine, asserting the right of the Soviet Union to take military action against any member of the socialist community in defence against domestic and foreign attempts to overthrow it, infuriated Chinese leaders. The implication of the corollary doctrine of 'limited sovereignty' was that the community of socialist states – led, of course, by the Soviet Union – had the right to determine the destiny of any community member.

China's domestic policies were also a source of friction in the late 1950s. China's delegate to the 20th CPSU Congress, Zhu De, stated that the socialist revolution would be completed on a nation-wide scale in China for the most part in some three years, while the following month Khrushchev castigated those in the Soviet Union who believed the advent of communism was at hand and that consumer goods production could therefore be given priority over heavy industry. By 1958 Chinese leaders were claiming to be able to leapfrog certain stages of economic and social development and thus reach the stage of communism more quickly. Khrushchev was alarmed and warned Chinese leaders about the dangers of the kind of economic experiment embodied in the policies of the Great Leap Forward. Yet Mao was suspicious of Khrushchev's motives, and experience of Moscow's niggardliness had already convinced Chinese leaders of the need to go it alone. Natural calamities, in particular bad weather, coupled with Soviet pressure throughout 1959 and into 1960, increased the determination of the Chinese to 'struggle against all odds'. Khrushchev decided to raise those odds when, as mentioned above, he decided in August 1960 to withdraw all Soviet and East European experts.

It was also at the 20th CPSU Congress that Khrushchev chose to de-emphasise the inevitability of war and seemed to extend the concept of 'peaceful co-existence' to the developed capitalist world, including the United States. Peking, on the other hand, appeared anxious for confrontation between the capitalist and communist camps, especially in the aftermath of the first successful Soviet test of an ICBM in August 1957, and the launching of the Sputnik in October of the same year. The tone of Mao Zedong's speech to representatives of Communist and Workers' Parties in Moscow on 18 November 1957 in which he proclaimed that the 'East wind prevails over the West wind' was in marked contrast to Khrushchev's more moderate stance and the 'Moscow Peace Manifesto'. Soviet inaction during the Taiwan Straits crisis in 1958, and Soviet policy during the Sino–Indian border conflict, the Cuban Missile Crisis and in signing the Nuclear Test Ban Treaty with Great Britain and the United States, further persuaded Chinese leaders that Moscow had set out upon a 'revisionist' course, and was no longer prepared to use its power to advance the aims of international communism.

The personal acrimony between Chinese and Soviet leaders – first between Mao and Stalin, and later between Mao and Khrushchev – was partly, at least, a result of the intractible nature of the differences between Moscow and Peking, but was also a byproduct of the competition between the leaders for influence in the international communist movement and, later, the enormous appeal of Maoism as an alternative model for socialist development. While it is difficult to assess precisely the degree or impact of such personal dislike, it is clear that the strained personal relations between Soviet and Chinese leaders did nothing to facilitate the resolution of Sino–Soviet differences. Chinese propaganda lashed out at 'Khrushchev revisionism' while Moscow viciously attacked 'Maoist adventurism', but relations between Moscow and Peking did not improve after the ousting of Khrushchev in 1964, and despite Soviet hopes of better relations in the post-Mao period, the new Chinese leaders have not responded favourably to Soviet overtures.

The period since Mao's death in September 1976 has, however, seen some significant changes in the Sino–Soviet relationship. There has been little improvement on the state-to-state front. Chinese leaders have no reason to believe the Soviet Union would prove a more reliable friend today than during the 1950s and 1960s. Soviet overtures following Mao's death have been in their eyes simply 'words without deeds' and the response from Peking has been cool-to-hostile. Soviet aid to Vietnam, which invaded Kampuchea in 1978–9, provided a new source of contention between Moscow and Peking, and the Chinese Government, which had in August 1978 concluded a treaty of friendship with Japan, announced in April 1979 that the Sino–Soviet Treaty of Friendship was no longer relevant. It was allowed to lapse in February 1980, and although Peking agreed to hold high-level talks on normalisation of state-to-state relations, the Soviet invasion of Afghanistan in December 1979 quickly brought them to a halt.

The border negotiations, which were to be kept separate, had continued intermittently since 1969. These had also proved unsuccessful, although the Chinese and Soviet governments had managed to resolve several practical problems involving river navigation in a separate set of talks – the Sino–Soviet joint commission for navigation on boundary rivers. The most significant development within this forum was the Soviet decision in October 1977 to lift its blockade of the main channel around Heixiazu/Bear Island. The gesture may, however, have been nothing more than a practical expedient since silting further upstream, turning the main navigational channel on to a course between the Chinese bank and a Chinese-held island, had given China the opportunity to apply reciprocal pressure by implicitly threatening a counter-blockade (Neville Maxwell, *The Times*, 29 September 1978 and *The Hindu* 30 September 1978).

The last few years have, however, seen some interesting developments on the ideological front. In early April 1980, an article in the *People's Daily* repudiated the so-called 'Nine Commentaries' which had marked the CPC's open break with the CPSU in 1963 and 1964. The Commentaries had labelled the Soviet Party 'revisionist' because of its emphasis on the development of productive forces. In Peking, 'Anti-Revisionism Street', on which the Soviet Embassy is located, reverted to the name it had before the Cultural Revolution – 'North Centre Street'. It is quite possible, however, that the admission on the part of Chinese leaders that the CPSU is no longer to be considered 'revisionist' has more relevance to Chinese domestic affairs and the implementation of new economic policies in China than to feelings about Moscow or Soviet overtures. Hu Yaobang, Secretary General of the CPC, said in that same month that China was firmly opposed to those parties 'that flaunt the Communist Party banner but in effect bully other parties, interfere with other countries' internal affairs, and even invade and occupy other countries' territory by force'. It appears, therefore, that so long as Soviet leaders adhere to the Brezhnev Doctrine, ideological differences – although redefined – will remain a stumbling block to the resumption of party-to-party relations.

As mentioned above, the personal factor is always difficult to isolate in the study of relations between states. In 1964, when Khrushchev was ousted as Prime Minister and First Secretary of the CPSU, Zhou Enlai travelled to Moscow to see whether an improvement in Sino–Soviet relations was possible. His talks with Soviet leaders proved fruitless. He returned to Peking and reported that there were no signs of a change in Soviet policy toward China. In September 1976, after the death of Mao Zedong, Soviet leaders, in a similar attempt to test the water, decided on a lull in anti-Chinese propaganda. Peking did not reciprocate and in April Soviet press attacks on China resumed. Chinese propaganda was however, directed less against particular Soviet leaders in the post-Khrushchev period. Soviet propaganda in the post-Mao period has continued to attack 'Maoism' and has argued that 'de-Maoisation' is a myth, but personal attacks on Chinese leaders have been rare. Thus, although Khrushchev's departure and Mao's death did not lead to an improvement in Sino–Soviet relations, their demises provided 'moments of opportunity' which for one reason or another were not seized upon, and did perhaps result in a diminution of the importance of the personal factor in the dispute.

Since Peking's hostility did not seem to be directed against Leonid Brezhnev – Khrushchev's successor – personally, but rather against Soviet policies, it seems unlikely that his passing will result in any significant change in the Sino–Soviet equation – unless, of course, it also results in policy changes which make the 'moment of opportunity' more meaningful. Such policy changes on the part of the post-Brezhnev leadership are unlikely, however, given the nature of Peking's demands and the depth of Soviet concern about 'the Chinese threat'.

Sino–Soviet relations are currently characterised by intermittent overtures from Soviet leaders declaring themselves ready to improve relations, Peking's coolness to such overtures and vehement criticism by Chinese leaders of Soviet 'hegemonism'. On 1 October 1977, a commentary in *Pravda*, signed 'I. Aleksandrov' – a pseudonym used to designate Soviet leading circles – marked the 28th anniversary of communist rule in China. It was coupled with a telegram to Peking from Soviet leaders expressing their interest in improving relations and urged China to settle the differences between the two countries. In February 1978, the presidium of the USSR Supreme Soviet sent a message to China's Fifth National People's Congress proposing talks between the Soviet Union and China to normalise their long-soured relations. Chinese leaders repeated preliminary conditions unacceptable to Moscow, but when it was announced in April 1979 that China intended to scrap the Sino–Soviet Treaty of Friendship, Peking dropped its pre-conditions and announced its willingness to discuss normalisation.

As we have seen, the normalisation talks came to nothing and were discontinued early in 1980. In April 'Aleksandrov' again called for efforts to resolve Sino–Soviet differences, saying that there were a number of possibilities for constructive solutions to the long-standing differences. In September, Moscow reaffirmed its willingness to establish better relations and said that it was up to Peking to reply. In response, Deng Xiaoping called on the Soviet Union to take 'concrete actions.' In his speech to the 26th CPSU Congress in February 1981, Brezhnev stressed the desire to build ties with China 'on a good neighbour basis.' In October 1981, the Soviet Government approached Peking with proposals to revive the border negotiations that were broken off in 1978. This time there were hints that Chinese leaders might be willing to resume such discussions.

In January 1982, Sergei L. Tikhvinsky, Director of the Soviet Academy of Foreign Affairs, had ten days of secret talks with Chinese officials in Peking, and in February Prime Minister Nikolai A. Tikhonov formally called for a resumption of talks on the border dispute. President Brezhnev himself appealed to China to end the two decades of hostility when he spoke in Tashkent in March, and on 20 May there was a further appeal from the pen of 'Aleksandrov'. The Chinese position appears to be that border negotiations should be resumed but that there is no hurry. In spite of the numerous Soviet appeals, Chinese leaders remain sceptical and are waiting to see whether Moscow offers any real concessions.

On 17 June 1981, the *People's Daily* carried a signed article entitled 'Where Lies the Crux of the Sino–Soviet Border Negotiations?' The article was quite specific as to Chinese objectives: first, Peking wants acknowledgement that 'treaties concerning the present Sino–Soviet boundary were unequal treaties imposed on China by tsarist Russian imperialism'; second, the Chinese government holds that the 'unequal treaties' should be taken as a basis for a peaceful settlement of the boundary question, and not the so-called 'historically formed' or 'actually guarded' line put forward by Moscow; third, territory occupied by either side in violation of those treaties should be returned, though adjustments may be made in consideration of the interests of the local inhabitants; fourth, a new and equal Sino–Soviet treaty should be signed – not a new unequal treaty under which more Chinese territory would be ceded to the Soviet Union; and fifth, the understanding reached by Prime Ministers Aleksei Kosygin and Zhou Enlai in 1969, which brought an end to the Amur-Ussuri fighting, should be implemented. It called for maintenance of the *status quo* along the border, the avoidance of armed conflict, and withdrawal of Soviet and Chinese forces from disputed areas.

In addition to the specific objectives relating to the Sino–Soviet frontier, Peking has also demanded that the Soviet Union withdraw its forces from Mongolia and from Afghanistan and compel its ally, Vietnam, to withdraw its forces from Kampuchea. In other words, Chinese leaders want to see a substantial change in Soviet foreign policy.

It would appear that Peking is waiting for an indication of Soviet willingness to concede some of these points before coming once again to the negotiating table. The Kremlin in 1969 simply denied that any agreement had been reached between the two Prime Ministers, and none of the more recent Soviet statements has shown even the slightest deviation from that stand or given the slightest hint of willingness to meet any of the Chinese 'preconditions'. The 20 May 'Aleksandrov' article complained:

when it comes to 'practical deeds', the leaders of the PRC are making a whole range of preliminary demands which the USSR must meet before any Soviet–Chinese talks begin. These include renunciation of support and assistance to the Mongolian People's Republic, the countries of Indochina and Afghanistan, the unilateral withdrawal of the Armed Forces of the Soviet Union from the border with the PRC, and recognition of China's 'rights' to vast areas of the USSR . . . the accumulation of all sorts of preliminary conditions bordering on ultimatums in no way testifies to the striving of the Chinese side to find a way out of the blind alley in which Soviet–Chinese relations are at the moment.

Moscow has alternatively proposed the conclusion of a treaty on the non-use of force and a non-aggression treaty, the holding of talks to normalise and improve state-to-state relations, and the drafting of a document on principles of relations between the two countries. Peking views such steps as meaningless verbiage if the Kremlin is not prepared to demonstrate its good will in a more concrete manner – by modifying either its policy with regard to the Sino–Soviet frontier or its foreign policy with regard to Kampuchea and Afghanistan. Soviet leaders, seeking some way to unravel the Sino–Soviet deadlock, have more recently decided to offer a carrot in the form of increased scientific and technological exchanges. While the resulting increase in Sino–Soviet contacts may produce a slightly better atmosphere, it is unlikely to be enough to tempt Peking to moderate its demands. Chinese leaders may respond to and accept the economic and technological carrot, but they will require something more substantial to draw them to the negotiating table. After all, they have had the experience of years of dialogue leading nowhere, and they know from experience that economic carrots can be quickly withdrawn.

It is unlikely that Andropov will be more willing to accede to Chinese demands than Leonid Brezhnev. While the Brezhnev leadership sometimes appeared to be split on certain questions – détente, trade with the West, policy towards East European satellites, etc. – no such schisms were apparent with regard to China, which is regarded almost universally as a serious threat to Soviet security. However Soviet Sinologists appear to hold differing views on the seriousness and nature of the 'Chinese threat', but such differences are not reflected in statements at the highest levels (see Garrett 1981). At first sight this seems rather curious since the Soviet Union is undoubtedly the stronger of the two militarily and economically, but Soviet leaders are alarmed by the trend toward economic and military cooperation between the West and China and fear that Peking may well succeed in its drive for modernisation. Even a relatively weak China on the Soviet Union's southern flank raises the possibility of a two-front confrontation in the event of war with the United States and its allies. And Peking's improvement of its nuclear arsenal with the addition of an ICBM and a presumed second-strike capability have rendered the option of a Soviet pre-emptive strike more problematic.

Moscow is also worried by adverse demographic trends which render the Soviet Far East, with its vast store of mineral wealth, vulnerable. Almost 80 per cent of the Soviet Union's primary energy reserves lie east of the Urals, although most of the energy is consumed in population centres in the European part of the country. The environment is extremely uninviting, making it difficult to attract Russian workers, and the local non-Russian inhabitants are not trusted by Soviet leaders for fear that Moscow's control over outlying regions and nationality groups may be threatened in the future. Such concern is not unreasonable, since the Russian people now constitute a bare majority within the Soviet Union with a much lower rate of population growth than that of the Muslim and Asian nationalities, and since Peking has recently shown keen interest in appealing to such groups.

Chinese leaders are aware of their country's relative economic weakness and have frequently expressed the hope for an extended period of peace during which priority can be given to the implementation of new economic policies. Military spending has been cut over the past two years and modernisation of China's armed forces is not considered as important as the other three of the 'four modernisations' – agriculture, industry, and science and technology. Still, the Kremlin is not totally convinced by the moderate visage of the post-Mao political scene. Moscow's hopes for a favourable response to its overtures have been dashed time and time again, and Soviet journals and articles have recently stressed that Chinese leaders are still following an aggressive and militaristic course. Soviet leaders apparently still feel that Peking hopes to remain aloof and profit from the 'fighting of the two tigers' (*Soviet News* 2 December 1980). Such propaganda is partly, of course, directed towards the West as a warning that befriending and aiding China may prove dangerous, but it reflects a real fear in Moscow that the kind of radicalism which made China an unpredictable power in the past may not have been totally eliminated.

Perhaps more worrying to Soviet leaders than the prospect of a direct military challenge from Peking or the revival of Chinese radicalism are Chinese activities and propaganda aimed at undermining Soviet interests in South and South-East Asia and Peking's growing co-operation with Japan. Moscow fears encirclement, with the establishment of an anti-Soviet front manipulated by Washington. In a *Pravda* article on 29 July 1980, Aleksandr Petrov said it was clear that 'China will try to harm the Soviet Union wherever it can and to the greatest possible extent'. He cited the evidence of 'China's aggression against Vietnam, responsibility for Pol Pot's crimes, armed provocations against sovereign Kampuchea and hostile acts against Laos, Burma, India, Afghanistan and other countries in the region'. Chinese leaders have, in fact, openly called for a united front against 'Soviet hegemonism'. While it is not always possible to obtain direct evidence of the extent of Peking's anti-Soviet, anti-Afghan, and anti-Vietnamese activities in South and South-East Asia, it is clear that Chinese leaders would wish the cost of Soviet occupation of Afghanistan and support for Vietnam to be as high as possible.

Soviet losses in Afghanistan have been high in human terms – an estimated 1200–1500 dead during the first year of fighting and countless others lost and wounded. Peking, which was extremely alarmed at the annexation of the Wakhan salient which 'pushes the Russian border right up to Pakistan' and at the armed intrusions of the Karmal regime's forces into Pakistan, is almost certainly aiding, training and arming Afghan rebels and refugees based in Pakistan. Soviet propaganda, however deliberately exaggerates the extent of Chinese–Pakistani co-operation and accuses China and Pakistan of plotting against India. An article in early February 1981 in *Sovetskaya Rossiya* accused China of building 12 airbases in Pakistan for use against India and said that Chinese troops were guarding a Pakistani nuclear centre where nuclear weapons are being developed. Thus Moscow attempts to divert attention from the real object of Peking's activities – opposition to Soviet occupation forces in Afghanistan – and to undermine Chinese and Pakistani initiatives to improve relations with India.

The cost of Soviet aid to Vietnam has also been high – an estimated US$3 million a day in 1980. In 1981 Moscow changed its policy governing assistance to Vietnam, demanding increased exports of rubber, timber, coffee, tea, fruit, handicraft articles and garments to the Soviet Union, in spite of painful shortages in the home market – further evidence that the burden of aid had become unacceptably high. Peking is in no hurry to resolve Sino–Vietnamese differences since a hungry, insecure Vietnam will continue to drain Soviet coffers. Chinese leaders hope that in time the Kremlin may decide to meet Chinese demands and press Vietnam to withdraw its forces from Kampuchea.

In the meantime, China has rejected Hanoi's proposals to resume stalled talks on reducing tension – talks begun in the aftermath of Peking's attempt to 'teach Vietnam a lesson' in February 1979, and has made increasing use of Vietnamese ethnic minorities in its border struggle with Vietnam. Peking has stepped up its campaign to poison the minorities against Hanoi and is using trained groups under the leadership of Mr Hoang Van Hoan – the former Vietnamese Politburo member who defected to China in 1979 – to carry out espionage, 'political sabotage' and psychological warfare. Chinese leaders thus hope to keep Vietnam unsettled at very little cost.

The Soviet Union has appealed to ASEAN to convene an ASEAN-Indochina regional conference on the problem of Kampuchea, but the ASEAN states have deemed the proposal 'unacceptable' as it 'seeks to justify and perpetuate the continued Vietnamese military occupation of Kampuchea'. Soviet propaganda consistently attempts to cast Peking in the role of 'aggressor' in South-East Asia, referring to China's 'list of claimed territories which includes ten million square kilometres of the territories of neighbouring countries', but it is clear that, for the moment, the ASEAN states are more concerned about the immediate threat of Soviet-backed forces poised on Thailand's doorstep.

Soviet leaders accuse China of attempting to enlist Japan in the 'anti-Soviet front' as well. The Kremlin was alarmed when, in August 1978, Peking concluded a treaty of peace and friendship with Tokyo – an achievement Moscow has been denied primarily because of its continued occupation of four Japanese islands taken during World War II. Soviet alarm has grown since Sino–Japanese relations have survived the temporary strain caused by Peking's economic 'readjustment' in 1981. On 20 July 1980, *Izvestiya* carried an article critical of Japan for 'joining in the game of creating a triangle consisting of the U.S., Japan and the PRC and directed against the Soviet Union and the individual countries of Asia', and Oleg Borisov, writing in *Kommunist* (no. 6/1981), stated that 'the activation of the political and military co-operation between Peking and Tokyo in the conditions of the present growth of militarist and revenge-seeking trends in Japan encouraged by the Chinese leadership, harbours a serious threat to peace in the Far East and to the security of all countries in that region'. Moscow has called for the establishment of a mutual security system of the countries in the region with the participation of China, Japan, the People's Democratic Republic of Korea and the United States and for 'confidence-building measures' in the Far East. Thus, Soviet leaders in each instance – with regard to the Sino–Soviet border, Afghanistan, Kampuchea and Japan – have sought to neutralise perceived threats to

Soviet interests, calling for measures to reduce tension, improve relations and increase co-operation. But Moscow remains determined to safeguard the *status quo*. Although negotiating from a position of strength, Soviet leaders appear preoccupied with the dangers facing the Soviet state and seem determined to maintain and bolster their buffer-state system. So long as there is no give on the Soviet side, the other parties are extremely unlikely to respond positively to the Kremlin's overtures.

Soviet perceptions of China are not, therefore, likely to change, but the feeling of insecurity on the part of the Soviet leaders – perhaps rooted in Russian history and most certainly enhanced by problems in Eastern Europe and Afghanistan – could, in a circuitous way, help to resolve the Sino–Soviet deadlock. It is conceivable that the new Soviet leadership might decide to use the 'moment of opportunity' available on its accession to retrench, as did the new Soviet leaders in the post-Stalin period when they concluded the Austrian State Treaty with the Western Powers in 1955 – the first significant withdrawal of Soviet power in Europe. If this is the case, such a move could be used as a lever to bring Chinese leaders to the discussion table. It is possible that Peking might be persuaded to enter into normalisation or border talks if Soviet forces began a withdrawal from Afghanistan or if Moscow cut back its aid to Vietnam. Such a move would result in an improved atmosphere, more state-to-state contacts and increased trade, but it is unlikely that such discussions would lead to any significant break-throughs or concessions on important points, since the demands and positions of both sides are so contradictory and so firmly fixed.

For their part, the Chinese leaders have appeared reluctant to use the 'Soviet card', even though the Reagan administration has for so long refused to accede to Chinese demands that weapons shipments to Taiwan be stopped and that Peking be acknowledged as the capital of 'one China'. It would appear that ruling circles in China feel that their aims of modernisation and economic growth would be imperilled without the support of the United States. Secret negotiations, during which Peking threatened to downgrade relations with the United States, have resulted in a communiqué in which Washington indicated that it would limit and gradually reduce arms deliveries to Taiwan. The fact that friendly Soviet overtures were not seized upon by Chinese leaders as a stick to beat Reagan with must have been reassuring to American officials.

It is impossible to predict with certainty the future course of Sino–Soviet relations since Soviet perceptions of insecurity could, as we have seen, elicit opposite reactions. On the one hand, Moscow may elect to maintain its current policy of 'protecting' neighbouring buffer territories and expanding its power and influence where it can, but on the other hand, Soviet leaders may decide that such actions actually weaken the Soviet Union by dissipating its strength. Similarly, the relaxation of Sino–American tensions following the recent joint communiqué may heighten Chinese resolve to insist that certain conditions be met before Sino–Soviet negotiations take place. On the other hand, the clarification of Washington's China policy may allow Chinese leaders to respond to Soviet invitations to talk without fear of alarming the powers-that-be in the U.S. Still, the Chinese have little to gain from rushing to the negotiating table, and when and if discussions are resumed, compromise will be difficult since, as we have seen, the positions of the two sides are so far apart. If, however, the change of leadership or a change in direction of Soviet foreign policy does allow an improvement in the Sino–Soviet relationship, it will be simply that – an improvement – not a *rapprochement*. There has really never been a Sino–Soviet friendship.

10 Is Détente Dead?
Hugh Seton-Watson

Détente means relaxation of tension between any pair or group of governments whose interests conflict. This is indeed the literal meaning of the expression *razryadka napryazhonnosti*, normally used in the Russian literature of the subject, whereas English language usage prefers a French word derived from the period when French was the internationally preferred language of diplomacy. 'Détente' in fact, as an abstract concept, has essentially the same meaning as 'appeasement', a word which in the late 1930s acquired, in the special historical conditions of the time, an unsavoury flavour. Considered in the abstract, both détente and appeasement are noble aims: it is when attempts are made to put them into practice that controversy begins.

Tension may be relieved in either of two ways: if each side to a conflict adopts a conciliatory posture, and makes substantial concessions to the other side; or if one side capitulates to the other. The second alternative is of course the optimum for the winning side, but does not usually benefit the loser. What was wrong with the 'appeasement' of the 1930s was precisely that Chamberlain made all the concessions – usually at the expense of third parties, his allies or dependents – while Hitler made all the gains. It is arguable that in the 1970s all the concessions – reduction of armaments programmes, abandonment of potentially important strategic positions and economic assistance to the other side – have been made by the United States, and that all the advantages have accrued to the Soviet Union.

There is a widespread belief that for some years past we have been living in a period of 'détente', which has replaced the earlier period of 'cold war'. This belief requires closer examination.

The expression 'cold war' came into general use soon after the end of the Second World War. Its invention is sometimes attributed to the American financier, Bernard Baruch, a close friend of President F.D. Roosevelt. Whether he was the author or not, it is certain that it was the American press which popularised the phrase, which was then adopted by most major languages of the world. The words 'cold war' denoted a state of affairs, a condition of the relations between governments. This was essentially the same as the condition described by Trotsky as 'neither peace nor war'. The antagonists in cold war do not fight each other directly. For the most part, they try to do every possible kind of mischief to each other, and give all possible support to each other's opponents, short of shooting.

However, shooting may take place between their proxies, usually in the form of a civil war. Some material help was given by the Soviet Union to the communists, and by the United States to the Kuomintang, in the Chinese civil war of the late 1940s. The Greek civil war of 1946–9, whose roots lay essentially in internal Greek conflicts, acquired an international character through the massive assistance given to the communists by Stalin's Albanian, Yugoslav and Bulgarian proxies, and to the government forces by the British and then by the Americans. In 1950 Stalin's proxies, the North Koreans, attacked the American proxies, the South Koreans. This soon brought to the aid of the South Koreans a United Nations force, dominated by Americans but including also British, Turks and a few others; and this in turn led to Chinese intervention on the North Korean side. The proxy war was brought to an end in 1953 on a *status quo ante* basis, which meant essentially that Stalin's enterprise had been defeated.

The war in Vietnam, lasting nearly twenty years, was also a proxy war. In the first stage proxies, materially aided by the Chinese, defeated the French. In the second stage, the Soviet proxies attacked American proxies, and this eventually brought in hundreds of thousands of Americans, whom the Soviet proxies, receiving massive material aid from the Soviet Union, eventually defeated. Unlike the Korean war, the Vietnam war ended in a Soviet victory, but in neither war did the Soviet leaders need to engage their own troops. From 1945 to 1980 we may say that Soviet policy adopted, with great success, the practice traditionally attributed, in the 18th and 19th centuries, to Britain, of fighting its wars with other countries' soldiers. The occupation of Afghanistan, and consequent guerrilla campaign, marked a new phase.

Cold war then was a state of affairs. The Second World War was succeeded not by peace, but by a condition of neither peace nor war, of cold war. These two words clearly and economically describe the reality.

Essentially, this state of affairs does not date from the late 1940s. From the beginning – ever since 1917 – the Soviet leaders have been at war with the 'capitalist world' and with 'imperialism'. This has an ideological aspect and a conventional foreign policy aspect.

According to Soviet doctrine, the human race is moving ineluctably towards socialism and communism. The only persons who can truly understand the past and present of this process, and can scientifically predict its future, are Marxist–Leninists. The only authentic, and indeed infallible, exponent of scientific Marxism–Leninism is the Central Committee (CC) of the CPSU, whose most authoritative spokesman is its Secretary General. The first socialist state in history was Soviet Russia, and the only socialists in the world are those who accept Soviet leadership. Socialism is what the CC of the CPSU says it is: nothing else is or can be. It is the duty of the Soviet leaders to help on the process of diffusion of socialism throughout the human race wherever and whenever they can. Marxist–Leninist wisdom however insists that unacceptable risks must not be taken; and indeed the wise men of the CC of the CPSU are by definition incapable of such folly – though they may sometimes make 'mistakes', and indeed it is now admitted that in Stalin's and Khrushchev's time a number of mistakes were made.

The conventional foreign aspect is equally important. The Soviet leaders in the 1920s genuinely feared an onslaught by the combined 'capitalist' powers. It was therefore an important part of their policy to exploit and to intensify any conflicts existing within the 'capitalist' world. The most important of these were the conflicts between Germany and her former victors France and Britain, between China wnd the European imperial powers, between Japan and the United States and between China and Japan. To oversimplify, one may say that the USSR supported Germany against the Western Powers from 1918 to 1934, the Western Powers against Germany from 1934 to 1939, Germany against Britain from 1939 to 1941, and Britain and the United States against Germany from 1941 to 1945.

After 1945 the world political scene became both simpler and more complicated. It was simpler because the old balance of power in Europe was destroyed by Soviet military predominance, half of Europe became part of a new Soviet empire and the other half (with the exception of a few small neutral states) became closely allied to the United States, which thereby restored the balance of power not on a European but on a world scale. Thus there was a single 'capitalist' or 'imperialist' enemy, and little room was left for diplomatic manoeuvring between individual European states, not one of which was a great power any more.

The world scene was also more complicated because there appeared outside Europe and North America a multitude of new states, emerging from a colonial condition, motivated by a love–hate relationship or by pure hatred towards their former rulers, uncertain of their identity, with unstable social structures and often quarrelling with each other. Added to the pre-existing small states of South and Central America (and the two big states of this region, Brazil and Mexico), they offered a rich variety of conflicts and aspirations to be exploited by 'scientific' purveyors of revolution. Stalin paid little attention to this new phenomenon, but his successors gave it a high priority, believing that gradual erosion and penetration of this Third World would transform the 'correlation of forces' (a favourite Soviet phrase) to the advantage of 'the socialist camp'.

Finally, the world scene was still more complicated by the unexpected conflict which developed in the 1960s between the Soviet Union and the People's Republic of China, as well as by the rise of Japan to be the third strongest economic power in the world. In contrast to Europe, it seemed possible that in the Pacific Basin at the end of the 20th century there might arise new balances of power between four great powers with great potential: United States, Soviet Union, China and Japan.

Throughout these changes in world politics during 60 years of the Soviet regime, the state of war between the Soviet Union and the rest of the world remained a fact. There were however three different types of situation.

The first may be described as unilateral cold war. The Soviet Union was at war with the rest, but the rest were not at war with it. During the inter-war years, the governments and the main political parties in Western countries undoubtedly disliked the Soviet regime, and from time to time some Western spokesman made some fiercely hostile speech. But enmity remained verbal. Western governments did little if anything, after the end of the much exaggerated intervention in the Russian Civil War in 1920, to harm the Soviet Union. This began to change in the mid-1930s when the Soviet leadership began to be seriously alarmed by the extremely hostile posture, impressive military preparations and successful territorial expansion of Hitler. Having tried alliance with France against Hitler and been disappointed, they then made an alliance with Hitler which kept them out of war for nearly two years, but left them without any possible help on the continent of Europe when Hitler attacked them in June 1941.

The second type of situation was a 'hot war', in which there were inescapable enemies – Hitler and his lesser allies – and in which help could eventually be obtained from allies – Britain, the United States and their lesser allies. From 1941 to 1945 there was a clear difference, from the Soviet point of view, between the immediate enemy and those who shared Soviet interest in defeating that enemy. Nevertheless, the basic attitude of the Soviet leaders to the wartime allies too remained one of continuing enmity. British and Americans, not only soldiers and workers but also political leaders, thought of the Soviet Union as a friendly power and Soviet citizens as friends. Similar feelings probably existed among simple Soviet citizens towards the American and British, but the leaders never relaxed their hostility.

The third type of situation was a bilateral cold war. Each side regarded the other as an enemy, but both sides avoided direct armed conflict with each other. This situation was uncomfortable for the Soviet Union, though Stalin on the whole managed it with a brilliant combination of bluff and caution. He would have much preferred to revert to a situation of unilateral cold war. Though he himself did not live to see it, this is what occurred under the leadership of his next two successors.

Imperceptibly but decisively, during the 1960s and 1970s, the words 'cold war' have changed their meaning. In English-language usage, they have ceased to denote a state of affairs, and have come to denote a policy, and a policy of which only Western 'capitalist' governments are capable. It is a policy of hostility towards the Soviet Union. Western spokesmen who impute discreditable motives to the Soviet government are 'cold warriors'. Soviet practitioners of international politics, or commentators on international affairs, are never cold warriors, and Soviet policy is never one of cold war. If Soviet spokesmen say unpleasant things about Western policies, or about the motives of Western statesmen, they are merely telling the truth, in their steadfast unfaltering pursuit of peace. This change was greatly to the Soviet advantage, but it was the result not of Soviet propaganda or subversion, but of Western wishful thinking.

The bad old Western policy of 'cold war', the blame for which Western 'liberals' increasingly imputed to the West, was associated with the names of Truman, Marshall, Acheson and Dulles. With the accession to power of Kennedy, there began to be talk on both sides of 'ending the cold war'. On both sides it was said that 'peaceful co-existence' was the desirable aim, and the word 'détente' came into more frequent use. Khrushchev and Kennedy made gestures to each other, and these were resumed soon after the Cuban missile crisis of 1962, which many have seen as the turning point from cold war towards détente. The continuing war in Vietnam limited the possibility of better relations, but did not diminish President Johnson's determination to improve his relations with the Soviet leaders by friendly gestures. The war was a suppurating sore in the American body politic, and it was to the Soviet interest that it should go on suppurating. The Soviet leaders could safely leave it to the American people to denounce its leaders and to tear its own society to bits. Meanwhile they could parade themselves from time to time as benevolent peace-loving statesmen. In Western Europe the pursuit of détente went ahead. Willy Brandt's *Ostpolitik* developed from its initial limited aim of reconciliation with Germany's eastern neighbours into a more far-reaching programme of co-operation, with undertones of neutralism. In France, the foreign policy of *Gaullisme* kept a careful balance between the United States and the Soviet Union, with rather more hostility to the first than to the second. In Britain, Harold Wilson constantly proclaimed his benevolence to all and sundry, giving a prominent place within his comprehensive embrace to the Soviet Prime Minister Kosygin, former henchman of Zhdanov and career-maker of the Great Purge, whom he publicly welcomed as having 'almost become part of the British way of life'.

'Détente' became the declared aim of American policy in the years of Nixon and Kissinger. It was pursued on both sides with considerable skill and consummate hypocrisy. The Soviet leaders made it very clear that in their concept of détente, the concessions should be made by the West. For their part, Nixon and Kissinger made frequent polite noises towards Moscow, but brought off the outstanding diplomatic success of the *rapprochement* with China. In these years, Soviet policy had at least two other major defeats. The first was the expulsion of Soviet advisers from Egypt by President Sadat in 1972. The second was the failure to prevent the Chinese–Japanese treaty of 1978, with its reference to 'hegemonism', the Chinese code-word for Soviet imperial expansion. This they might have prevented if they had been willing to return two islands of the Kurile chain to Japan. But the Soviet leaders appear to have adopted as their guiding principle the statement of Emperor Nicholas I in 1850, when informed that a Russian naval officer had established a Russian post on the coast of the Sea of Okhotsk which until then had been of no interest to him: 'Where the Russian flag has been raised, it shall never be lowered'. For 'Russian flag' substitute 'flag of socialism', bearing in mind that 'socialism' means 'what the CC of the CPSU says is socialism'.

Kissinger's grasp of the realities of Soviet policy cannot be questioned. His aim was to combine the rhetoric of détente with the practice of cold war, to see to it that the important concessions were made by the other side. However, he was unable to do all that he wished, because he was limited by the illusions of the American public, misled by the widespread misunderstandings of the concepts of 'détente', 'cold war' or 'peaceful co-existence', and demoralised by the traumatic effects of the Vietnam war.

It is an essential part of the Soviet doctrine of 'détente' that it is in no way incompatible with active support to the forces of 'national liberation'. It is of course for the CC of the CPSU, in the person of its Secretary General, to decide whether any given movement is, or is not, one of 'national liberation'. The Hungarian workers in 1956, the Polish workers of 'Solidarity' in 1980–81, or the advocates of Ukrainian or Lithuanian independence emphatically do not deserve this description: they are traitors to the working class, or bourgeois nationalists, or plain fascists. In Afghanistan, the forces of 'national liberation' are the group led by Babrak Karmal: the Afghan insurgents against his rule are agents, conscious or unconscious, of imperialism. In short, 'national liberation' movements are any groups which are both hostile to the United States or its allies, and efficient enough to be able, given Soviet support, to damage US interests and to tie down men or resources. In the Soviet view, if the Soviet government supports any such anti-Western activity anywhere, it is not thereby contradicting its avowed policy aim of 'détente'; but if any Western government supports any activity unwelcome to the Soviet government, it is offending against 'détente'. 'Détente' means relaxation of tension on the part of Western governments by surrendering to Soviet policies: unilateral concessions by the West.

No one understood this better than Kissinger; but he was unable to persuade the US Congress or the US public to support Angolan guerrillas opposed to the Cuban-officered Soviet proxy forces of the MPLA, or the Eritrean or Somali opponents of the Cuban- or East-German-officered forces of the Ethiopian Colonel Mengistu. The prevalent view of the US Congress, the American 'liberal' press and predominant public opinion in the German Federal Republic, France and Britain was that 'détente' required continued acquiescence by the West in Soviet expansion, continued economic concessions by the West to the Soviet Union, and above all, no competitive rearmament in the face of the steadily growing Soviet military and naval power. In this climate of opinion, Kissinger could only maintain a cautious rearguard action.

With the election of President Carter, helpless realism was replaced by divided counsel. Security Adviser Brzezinski had approximately the same basic view of Soviet policy as Kissinger, and favoured appropriate resistance, though not on precisely the same lines as his predecessor. In the State Department, the tendency was the greatest forbearance towards the Soviet Union, in the often repeated but never yet fulfilled hope that kindness and courtesy in Washington would produce kindness and courtesy in Moscow. In the President's own immediate entourage there was still greater optimism, and persons with little knowledge of foreign or defence policy pressed for acquiescent policies for reasons of internal politics. In the fourth year of Carter's term, came the Soviet invasion of Afghanistan, which gave rise to floods of denunciatory rhetoric but little action. Carter was also cursed, and Brezhnev blessed, with a phenomenon for which neither was in the least responsible, Ayatollah Khomeini. During Carter's last year as president, the policy of the greatest power in the world was paralysed by the blackmailing antics of a group of man-hunting brigands.

By the time that Reagan became President, the world 'détente' had become unpopular in the United States, though it still aroused favourable reactions in Western Europe, including Britain. It is difficult for an outside observer to guess what the foreign policy of the Reagan administration is, or indeed whether it has one. A good deal of rhetoric emerges from Washington, the main emphasis being on the failure of the European allies to support the United States. Corresponding rhetoric from Europe, especially from the German Federal Republic, puts the blame on the United States, especially its economic and military policies. Probably both sides were right: each had a great deal to blame the other for. However, it was sad to note that the main effect of the continuing guerrilla war in Afghanistan and the military *coup d'état* against Solidarity in Poland was to produce a trans-Atlantic slanging match.

From this survey, it would appear that cold war and détente have not differed very much from each other in practice. Basic Soviet attitudes have remained unchanged, and so have Soviet aims – extending in the long term to the limits of the earth, in the short term, highly flexible and sometimes very limited. Western attitudes, at the official level, have fluctuated considerably, but there has been a minimum continuity of suspicion and caution. At the level of public opinion in the West, extreme optimism and wishful thinking have welled up from time to time, and these have had a feedback on the policy-makers, often seriously limiting their freedom of manoeuvre. This type of constraint on policy-making is hardly visible on the Soviet side. The result of public pressures and official caution in the West has been a constant tendency to revert to unilateral cold war, with Western official awareness and unease not accompanied by effective action.

To anyone who thinks seriously about international affairs, the prospect of an unending condition of neither war nor peace is bleak, and indeed seems morally unacceptable. It is not only to Western minds that this seems so. Perhaps the most eloquent spokesman for a contrary view has been a Soviet citizen, the eminent scientist, Academician A.D. Sakharov. In Sakharov's view, the great worldwide problems of poverty, overpopulation and pollution, all of which were growing more acute with every passing year, and all of which could be handled only by close co-operation between governments, and especially between the governments of the world's two most powerful states, far outweighed the doctrinaire arguments about the merits or faults of 'capitalism' and 'socialism', and reduced to triviality the dogmas of the 'rivalry between two social systems'. But his arguments made no impression on the Soviet leaders, who persisted in their belief in the irreconcilable conflict between the forces of 'socialism' (identified in practice as the forces of the Soviet empire and its dependencies) and 'imperialism' (identified as the United States and all regions and all peoples associated with or controlled by them). Even when they adopted a more conciliatory tone in specific dealings with the 'imperialists', there was no change in the view of the present and future world which they offered to their own subjects, nor in their determination to exploit any troubles anywhere in the world against their adversaries.

The most appropriate form of such exploitation would depend on the circumstances of each case. In Afghanistan, large Soviet military forces were committed; in Ethiopia, a small number of Soviet military advisers, supplemented East German advisers and Cuban troops.

Muslim fanaticism in Iran or further west was best left alone, among other reasons because of its possible effects on the 40 million plus Muslims in the Soviet Union. It was wiser to rely on Arab hostility to Israel, and the commitment of the United States to Israel, to do their work for them. Whatever might be his own individual view, no Arab ruler could dare argue publicly that the Soviet Union was a more serious and longer-term menace to Arab and other Muslim nations than was Israel. In Latin America, the Soviet leaders could count on hostility to the United States to operate to their advantage. In the Falklands war, their posture to the outside world was restrained, though the tone of the 'anti-imperialist' invective addressed to the Soviet public was not. Whatever might be the view of individual Latin American leaders about Argentine behaviour, none could dare not to blame Anglophone 'colonialists' and not to denounce the all-purpose scapegoat for all woes of South America, the 'imperialists' beyond the Rio Grande. All that was required of Soviet diplomacy, and of Soviet agents in Latin America, was to help sharpen the tone of the rhetoric.

Western thinking, as reflected in the mass media and in the speeches of politicians, is often obfuscated by false dichotomies, by unreal 'either–or' alternatives. One such is between 'negotiation' and 'confrontation'. To some on the extreme right the word 'negotiation' appears as a synonym for capitulation. It is a curious kind of defeatism which assumes that in any negotiation one will always be outsmarted by the adversary. It is also a curious conception of the relations between governments that holds that one should only enter into negotiation with the virtuous, and that if a government has committed some act of which one disapproves, one should punish it by refusing to speak to it. There will always be matters for negotiation, especially for two governments whose interests and influence encompass the whole world.

But blindness, or faulty vision, on this subject is not confined to the extreme right. There is a corresponding 'liberal' fallacy which holds that if one negotiates, one must refrain from policies which the other side regards as hostile. For example, during arms control negotiations, one's own armaments programme must be held back. The Soviet leaders have never had such inhibitions. While negotiating on specific problems with Western governments they have continued their massive armaments programmes, their massive 'anti-imperialist' propaganda effort at home and abroad and their assistance to such anti-Western political movements – armed or unarmed – as seemed to offer opportunities. Long-term implacable hostility, and the deep conviction that the 'socialism' of which they are the sole infallible representatives will inevitably triumph over 'capitalism', and can and should be accelerated by their own action at suitable moments, can co-exist in the minds of Soviet negotiators with a willingness to discuss specific problems in an amiable manner, and even to make small concessions when this seems necessary.

Experienced Western negotiators are, of course, fully aware of this, and themselves operate on the two levels, viewing long-term Soviet policy with extreme distrust – though not pursuing a sustained effort to overthrow the Soviet regime, or Soviet imperial rule over other nations in Europe or Asia – and at the same time conducting practical business in an amiable manner. However, thinking on two levels is beyond the power of most Western media and politicians, let alone of the general public. Constant use and misuse of such phrases as 'end of the cold war', 'détente' and 'peaceful co-existence' create the illusion that Soviet hostility is a thing of the past, that friendly relations have become possible if only, by unilateral concessions, the Western governments can persuade the Soviet leaders of their good will. Western diplomats seldom fall prey to these illusions, but inevitably widespread public illusions have a feedback upon the political situation, and weaken them in their negotiations. No corresponding pressure exists on the Soviet side, since the Soviet government is not obliged to pay attention to Soviet public opinion on foreign affairs, and in any case the Soviet public is kept in a condition of hostility and suspicion towards the 'capitalist' countries by an unending stream of internal propaganda, which admits of no contradiction.

The Soviet concept of 'détente' envisages an unending series of concessions and surrenders by the West, unmatched by any but minor temporary tactical retreats from the Soviet side. The Soviet leaders would much prefer peaceful Western capitulation by stages to any kind of confrontation. Western governments have found it very difficult not to play the détente game by Soviet rules, very largely because of the pressure of their own publics. Boring reiteration of the hard facts about Soviet policy does not go down well with Western public opinion, which expects change, variety and quick results. The result is that the effective practical interpretation of 'détente' in the 1980s is very like that of 'appeasement' in the 1930s.

Yet true détente – reduction of tension by concessions on both sides – must remain the aim of policy. To assume that because true détente is not in sight, it is idle to aim at it, is defeatism. Academician Sakharov's way is the right way. To accept harsh realities is the necessary task of diplomats and politicians: statesmanship sets its sights higher. From time to time in history, break-throughs of statesmanship do occur. We must hope that the years ahead will be of this kind, even if today no gap is visible in the dark clouds.

The answer to the question which was put to me, and which forms the title of this essay, is simple. Détente is not dead: it has not yet been born.

References

Birman, I. 1978, 'From the achieved level', *Soviet Studies*, April

Birman, I. 1980, 'The financial crisis in the USSR', *Soviet Studies*, January

de Boer, S.P. *et al*. 1982, *Biographical Dictionary of Dissidents in the Soviet Union*, The Hague, Martinus Nijhoff

Borisov, O.B. and B.T. Koloskov, 1975, *Soviet–Chinese Relations 1945–1970*, Indiana University Press

Breyev, B.D. 1979, *Methods of Planning Employment in the USSR*, trans., Central Books

Brown, A.H. 1980, 'The power of the General Secretary of the CPSU' in T.H. Rigby *et al*. (eds) *Authority, Power and Policy in the USSR*, London, Macmillan

Brzezinski, Z. 1967, *The Soviet Bloc: Unity and Conflict*, Harvard University Press.

Checinski, M. 1982a, *Poland: Communism, Nationalism, Anti-Semitism*, New York.

Checinski, M. 1982b, 'Terror und kommunistische Politik in Polen', *Osteuropa*, vol. 32, no. 9

Chernenko, K.U. 1978, *Nekotorye voprosy tvorcheskogo razvitiya stilya partiinoi i gosudarstvennoi raboty*, Moscow

Danilov, L. 1981, *The Eleventh Five Year Plan*, Moscow, Progress Publishers

Dawisha, K. and P. Hanson (eds) 1981, *Soviet–East European Dilemmas: Coercion, Competition and Consent*, London, Heinemann Educational Books

Dawisha, K. and A. Dawisha (eds) 1982, *The Soviet Union in the Middle East: Policies and Perspectives*, London, Heinemann Educational Books

Ellman, M.J. 1969, *Soviet Planning Today*, Cambridge University Press

Fallenbuchl, Z.M. 1970, 'The communist pattern of industrialisation', *Soviet Studies*, April

Gardner, H.S. 1979, 'The factor content of Soviet foreign trade: a synthesis', *ACES Bulletin*, Summer

Garrett, B. 1981, *Soviet Perceptions of China and Sino–American Military Ties: Implications for the Strategic Balance and Arms Control*, Washington DC, The Pentagon

Gati, C. (ed) 1976, *The International Politics of Eastern Europe*, New York, Praeger

Gilberg, T. 1981, 'The political order', in S. Fischer-Galati, (ed)*Eastern Europe in the 1980s*, Boulder, CO., Westview Press

Gomulka, S. 1976, 'Soviet post-war industrial growth', in Z.M. Fallenbuchl, *Economic Development in the Soviet Union and Eastern Europe*, vol. 2, New York, Praeger

Hanson, P. 1981, *Trade and Technology in Soviet–Western Relations*, London, Macmillan

Hodnett, G. 1975, 'Succession contingencies in the Soviet Union', *Problems of Communism*, no. 2, March–April

Holzman, F.D. 1979, 'Some systemic factors contributing to the convertible currency shortages of CPE's', *American Economic Review*, May

Jones, C.D. 1981, *Soviet Influence in Eastern Europe: Political Autonomy and the Warsaw Pact*, New York, Praeger

Kende, P. *et al*. (eds) 1982, *Le système communiste: un monde en expansion*, Paris, IFRI

Kissinger, H. 1979, *The White House Years*, London, Weidenfeld & Nicolson

Kissinger, H. 1982, *Years of Upheaval*, London, Weidenfeld & Nicolson

Lavigne, M. 1980, 'L'URSS dans le Comecon face à l'Ouest' in *Strategies des pays socialistes dans l'échange internationale*, Paris, CNRS

Lewin, M. 1975, *Political Undercurrents in Soviet Economic Debates*, London, Pluto Press

Meissner, B. 1981, 'The 26th Party Congress and Soviet domestic policies', *Problems of Communism*, no. 3, May–June

Nove, A. 1981, 'The Soviet industrial enterprise', in I. Jeffries (ed) *The Industrial Enterprise in Eastern Europe*, New York, Praeger

Rakowska-Harmstone, T. 1976, 'Towards a theory of Soviet leadership maintenance' in P. Cocks *et al*. (eds) *The Dynamics of Soviet Politics*, Cambridge, MA, Harvard University Press

Scanlan, A.F.G. 1981, 'The Effects of energy development on East European economic prospects' in *Economic Reforms in Eastern Europe and Prospects for the 1980s*, Brussels, NATO

Smith, A.H. 1982, 'Soviet trade with the Middle East', in K. Dawisha and A. Dawisha (eds), op cit.

Stern, J.P. 1982, *East European Energy and East–West Trade in Energy*, London, Royal Institute of International Affairs

Sutton, A.C. 1968–71, *Western Technology and Soviet Economic Development*, 3 vols, Stanford, CA, Hoover Institution

Szporluk, R. (ed) 1976, *The Influence of Eastern Europe and the Soviet West on the USSR*, New York, Praeger

Szűcs, J. 1981, 'Vázlat Európa három történeti régiójáról', *Történelmi Szemle*, no. 3

US CIA 1979, *Energy Supplies in Eastern Europe A Statistical Compilation*, Washington DC

Vneshnyaya 1981a, *torgovlya v 1980g.*, Moscow

Vneshnyaya 1981b, *torgovlya SSR za 1971–1980 gg.*, Moscow

Voslensky, M. 1980, *Nomenklatura: Die herrschende Klasse der Sowjetunion*, Munich, Verlag Fritz Molden

Index

grain embargo, 63–4
investment in Soviet Armed
    Forces, 111, 114, 116–18
level of control in Eastern
    Europe, 9, 23, 121, 126,
    128
Machine Tractor Stations
    (MTS), 92
Politburo, 20–22, 26, 29, 31, 42
relations with Africa, 3, 25
    with Bulgaria, 123–4
    with Central Asia, 41, 51–2
    with China, 9, 10, 22–4,
        129–42, 146, 148
    with Czechoslovakia, 23,
        121, 123
    with Eastern Europe, 7, 100,
        125, 128, 141
    with the Federal Republic of
        Germany, 45, 52, 149
    with France, 145–7, 149
    with Hungary, 120, 132
    with Poland, 23, 35, 55, 57
    with the UK, 145–6, 149
    with the US, 9, 23, 35, 52,
        64, 133, 138, 140
    with Vietnam, 134, 137, 141
the Secretariat, 28, 30, 32, 42
the Secretary General, 1, 31,
    45, 148
Soviet Armed Forces, 112–13,
    115–18
the Supreme Soviet, 16, 31, 42,
    135
technology, 5, 7, 62, 73, 75, 81,
    97, 123
trade policy, 103
trade with the East, 8, 104–06,
    109–10
trade with the West, 8, 63–4,
    100, 102, 104, 106–10
Stalin, J.V., 2, 3, 5, 12–17, 22–3,
    30, 33, 35–7, 41, 54, 68, 69,
    81, 90, 109–10, 130, 132–3,
    144–6
Stalin, S., 42

Suslov, M., 20, 28, 43
Sweden, 44–5

Taiwan, 131, 133, 141
Technology, 5, 7, 62, 73, 75, 81,
    97, 123
Thailand, 140
The Third World, 67, 76,
    116–17, 129, 145
Tikhonov, N.A., 20, 31, 37, 39,
    136
Tikhvinsky, S.L., 136
Titov, V.N., 19
Transcaucasia
    nationalist movement in, 41,
        46, 50, 53
Transylvania, 125
Treaty of Friendship between
    China and the Soviet Union,
    130, 134–5
Trotsky, L.D., 36, 143
Truman, H., 147
Tsvigun, S., 43, 55
Tupolev, 97
Turkey, 50
Turkmenistan, 44, 51
Tvardovsky, A., 54

Ukraine
    nationalist movement in, 6, 20,
        27, 32, 41, 46–8, 54, 58
United Kingdom
    relations with China, 133
    relations with the Soviet
        Union, 145–6, 149
    trade with the Soviet Union, 64
United States of America
    economic relations with the
        Soviet Union, 62, 71, 73,
        75
    involvement in Vietnam, 2
    military relations with the
        Soviet Union, 3, 113–16,
        118
    relations with China, 141, 144
    relations with Japan, 145